TEACHING PHYSICALLY HANDICAPPED CHILDREN

Methods and Materials

TEACHING PHYSICALLY HANDICAPPED CHILDREN

Methods and Materials

——— *By* ———

HAROLD D. LOVE, Ed.D.

Professor of Special Education
University of Central Arkansas
Conway, Arkansas

CHARLES C THOMAS · PUBLISHER
Springfield · Illinois · U.S.A.

Published and Distributed Throughout the World by
CHARLES C THOMAS • PUBLISHER
BANNERSTONE HOUSE
301-327 East Lawrence Avenue, Springfield, Illinois, U.S.A.

© *1978, by* CHARLES C THOMAS • PUBLISHER
ISBN 0-398-03703-5
Library of Congress Catalog Card Number: 77-22317

With THOMAS BOOKS *careful attention is given to all details of
manufacturing and design. It is the Publisher's desire to present
books that are satisfactory as to their physical qualities and artistic
possibilities and appropriate for their particular use.* THOMAS
BOOKS *will be true to those laws of quality that assure a good
name and good will.*

Printed in the United States of America
N-1

Library of Congress Cataloging in Publication Data

Love, Harold D
    Teaching physically handicapped children.

    Bibliography: p.
    Includes index.
    E. Physically handicapped children—Education.
2. Teaching—Aids and devices.   I. Title.
LC4215.L68 1977   371.9'1   77-22317
ISBN 0-398-03703-5

PREFACE

THIS book is intended to be a combination text and resource book in methods and materials. As such, it treats the behavior of physically handicapped children and describes approaches to evaluation, description, and education. The position of the author is that the consequences of evaluation should be educational planning and postschool training. These functions are included in the concept of methods and material. To be specific, methods and material refers to the combination of theoretical and empirical functions that contribute to the physically handicapped child's education.

Although most physically handicapped children are educated in the regular classroom, it is the belief of the author that special methods and materials should be employed to aid these students. Hopefully, this book will meet those needs.

H.D.L.

ACKNOWLEDGMENTS

NO AUTHOR is unaided; therefore, what has evolved into the materials presented in this book has been influenced by many people who deserve recognition. Miss Rita Weny, Director of the Orthopedic Wing of Henderson Junior High School, Little Rock, Arkansas, deserves special recognition for her advice and materials. Gail James, Susan Galloway, Barby Libby, Gay Easby-Smith, and Joyce Bradley deserve special thanks for many contributions toward the making of this book. The author should like to single out Jean Thompson not only for typing the manuscript, but for editing and rewriting many passages. Joe Walthall contributed, as did Mary Kathryn Stewart.

H.D.L.

CONTENTS

TEACHING PHYSICALLY HANDICAPPED CHILDREN

Methods and Materials

Chapter 1

OVERVIEW OF ORTHOPEDIC HANDICAPS, TRAUMATIC HEALTH CONDITIONS, AND SENSORY DEFECTS

THIS chapter deals with orthopedic handicaps, traumatic health conditions, and sensory defects; cerebral palsy has been omitted from this chapter. This condition is covered in Chapter 5.

ORTHOPEDIC HANDICAPS

Juvenile Rheumatoid Arthritis

Although rheumatoid arthritis may appear in children, it is most likely to be present in adults. It is estimated that about 250,000 children are affected in the United States by this condition. Rheumatoid arthritis is brought on by inflammation of the joints; the etiology of this inflammation is unknown. It is believed by researchers that this inflammation is caused by an immunologic attack against normal body materials. This condition is not considered to be inherited, but occasionally it does affect several members of one family.

A peculiarity of rheumatoid arthritis in children is that approximately 60 to 75 percent of them will be free of all symptoms after a period of ten years. Most authorities agree that all therapy must be performed with the thought in mind that a remission will occur. No one can say how long a particular child will have the disease, but it will be months or even years.

There are three types of juvenile rheumatoid arthritis—*systemic, polyarticular,* and *pauciarticular.* With the systemic type, the child often has a high fever once or twice a day, enlarged lymph nodes, and a large spleen. He is often tired and fatigues quite easily. The physical conditions of the systemic type are minimal, but many of these children develop polyarticular arthritis. Very often, these children are admitted to the hospital to rule out more serious diseases, such as cancer. Of children having juvenile rheumatoid arthritis, 50 to 60 percent have the polyarticular type. These children may have fever, rash, anemia, etc., but they all have severe joint problems. The joints most frequently involved are those in the following order: knees, ankles, wrists, neck, fingers, elbows, shoulders, hips, and jaw. These children are in constant pain and need medical treatment a large portion of the time. Children with polyarticular arthritis often have permanent damage.

With pauciarticular arthritis, the child usually has three or fewer swollen joints during the first few months of the disease. Also, the child with this type generally does not have permanent damage. The most serious problem in this type is inflammation of the iris and the controlling muscles of the lens of the eye.

Arthrogryposis Multiplex Congenita

Arthrogryposis is a congenital condition whereby children are born with weak muscles and/or stiff joints. The cause of this condition is not known, but it is known that the process begins in the fetal stage of development. As stated above, it is not known why but the muscles in the fetus fail to function properly, and this lack of early movement probably causes the joints to be stiff and even causes some deformities in the limbs of the fetus and, later, the child.

Types and Symptoms

There are two types of arthrogryposis (ar-throw-gry-po-siss): *neuro–* and *myopathic*. Bleck (1975) states the consensus among medical people is that the myopathic form is probably a different disease and therefore can be discounted. The neuropathic type causes the children to resemble marionettes, and the limbs are fixed in a particular position, but the most typical picture is that of a child with flexed stiff elbows, flexed wrists and fingers, and stiff knees. The following characteristics of children with the neuropathic form are presented by Bleck (1975):

Shoulders are turned in.
Elbows are straightened.
Forearms are turned with the palm down (pronated).
Wrists are flexed and deviated inward.
Fingers are curled into the palms.
Hips are bent upward (flexed) and turned outward (externally rotated).
Knees are either bent or straightened.
Feet are usually turned in and down (equinus and varus).
Spine often shows curvature (scoliosis).
Limbs are small in circumference.
Joints appear larger and have loss of motion.
Skin is frequently dimpled over joints that are fixed in extension.
Intelligence and speech are usually normal.

Generally, arthrogrypotis children are deformed and crippled and have very little joint movement. Sometimes they can walk, but usually they must use a wheelchair and often have associated conditions, such as heart disease, abdominal hernias, respirator problems, and several different facial abnormalities.

Educational Implications

These children should have normal educational treatment, because the majority have normal or above normal intelligence and normal speech. There will, of course, be a need for special treatment in the classroom, because the child is crippled and the regular classroom teacher will have to take care of some of the special needs of this child as well as teach him. If physically handicapped children have average or above intelligence, they can be educated in the regular classroom, as opposed to a special class for physically handicapped children.

TRAUMATIC HEALTH CONDITIONS

A *trauma,* in medical terms, is an injury or wound violently produced and the condition or resultant neurosis. In psychiatric terms, it is an emotional experience or shock that has a lasting psychic effect (Webster's Dictionary, 1959). This chapter considers several medical conditions occurring during childhood and the associated medical and/or psychiatric traumas. The conditions include burns, amputations, Legg-Calvé-Perthes disease (also known as *osteochondrosis*), spinal curvature, and multiple sclerosis. Implications of the disease or condition and the concomitant trauma will depend, to a large extent, on the age and state of emotional and physical development of the child. Consequently, attention first will be given to normal stages of growth and development in childhood. Next, the specific conditions will be detailed, along with the impact they have on the lives of children. Each condition has specific implications for children at home and in school. Some involve chronic illness, and others demand emergency care; these areas will both be considered.

Parents play a very important role in every aspect of the lives of their children. How they can be most helpful and helped during their child's illness or infirmity will be discussed. Medical personnel also play an important role, and attention will be given to how they can be most effective. The impact of the child's stay in the hospital may have lifetime effects and will be treated with suggestions of researchers on how it can be managed with minimum pain and frustration for the child and, hopefully, everyone else in the environment.

Stages of Development

Much attention has been given to descriptions of the progressive stages of children in the course of their development from birth through adolescence. The descriptions of Piaget (Petrillo and Sanger, 1972) of how children think and of Ilg and Ames (1964) of behavior at various ages can be used to provide a composite of expectations of the child as he grows and matures. This information can be useful to the professional and reassuring to the parent, both of whom may be baffled from time to time by a child's actions.

From birth until two years of age, according to Piaget, the child is primarily involved in sensorimotor development. According to Ilg and Ames, the one-year-old can crawl and walk and is beginning to be sociable with strangers. At eighteen months, the child tends to have boundless energy and becomes somewhat more disagreeable. By two years, the child is more secure in his motor development and able to defer gratification momentarily. Piaget describes the two-year-old as having attained relatively coherent organization of his sensorimotor action and involved in egocentric thinking. The two-and-one-half-year-old child, according to Ilg and Ames (1964), again becomes contrary and demanding, displaying violent emotions.

To Piaget, three to seven years are the ages of preoperational thought, when thinking is intuitive and prelogical. Ilg and Ames describe the three-year-old as being very social and having good equilibrium and greater motor ability. The three-and-one-half-year-old again feels insecure and uncoordinated while the four-year-old is totally "out of bounds" in every way. Four-and-one-half brings greater control and awareness of others in the world, and five is an age of extreme equilibrium. Six is another age of violent emotions and rigid negativism, resulting in a relatively quiet and withdrawn seven-year-old.

Piaget considers seven to twelve years the years of concrete operational thought. Ilg and Ames describe eight-year-olds as expansive and busy, nine-year-olds as more sure of themselves and also potentially more neurotic, and ten as an age of predictable, comfortable equilibrium.

The child suffering from an illness or accident endures the trauma very differently, according to his age and maturity. The inability of the young child to express pain and localize symptoms makes it more crucial for medical personnel to be alert for other than verbal indications (Haller, 1973). The trauma may affect the child during several stages in his development. His disorder is seen while his personality is still developing; therefore, the manifestations of the disorder are more undifferentiated than in adults, and the clinical picture may vary greatly according to the child's age (Seligman, 1974).

Children sometimes see pain as punishment for something they have done wrong. This feeling is stronger in the younger child. Repeated reassurance by those around can help. Children may regress as their response to pain: The regression may take the form of angry outbursts or refusals to eat. Hospital personnel can accept and understand this behavior as normal under the circumstances and explain the phenomenon to the parents. Sometimes, the lack of an aggressive reaction to pain can be an indication of a more deeply involved emotional problem, and psychiatric consultation may be needed (Long and Cope, 1961). In the case of a serious trauma, a burn, for example, the prognosis is often better for the older child, who is more able to understand and cope with what is happening to him (Seligman, 1974).

Burns

Burns are second only to transportation accidents as a cause of accidental death to children. Each year 2000 children in the United States die as a result of burns (Randolph et al., 1974). Burns may be caused by chemical, electrical, actinic, or thermal injury. Thermal injuries are most frequent in the young (Holt et al., 1962). Scalds and flame burns are the most common thermal injuries. Other causes of burn injury include explosions, house fires, high-voltage electrical injury, and caustic liquids coming in contact with the skin. Of the two major groups of thermal burns, scald burns occur most frequently to infants and young toddlers and flame burns to curious older children (Randolph et al., 1974).

Management

The management of the burn patient is essentially the same regardless of the cause. For minor burns, considered first or second degree, treatment involves five stages. The first step is to allay the initial pain. The second step is to prevent shock from fluid loss. Next, infection must be prevented, and last, repair is promoted. Nutrition of the severely burned patient is an important consideration, and steps must be taken to insure an adequate intake of protein and calories during convalescence (Holt et al., 1962). The burned child may be treated with topical antibiotics and supportive intravenous care at first. Later comes débridement under a general anesthetic, and grafting if necessary, is done at the appropriate time.

The goal in the care of the burned child is to return the child to his home when he is able to move all his joints, has minimal scarring and disfigurement, and is undergoing a vigorous program of psychological and physical rehabilitation.

The post burn time period for the child can be divided into four stages. The first stage is the shock phase when the child arrives at the hospital and is grossly cleaned. The second stage is the period of vulnerability to infection, the third is the stage of malnutrition and infection, and the fourth stage is rehabilitation (Randolph et al., 1974).

Rule of Nines

The percentage of the body burned and the full thickness of the burn are important factors and are determined by a simplified method called the *rule of nines,* developed by Pulaski and Tennyson. Each arm is 9 percent; each leg, 18 percent; the posterior trunk, 18 percent; the anterior trunk, 18 percent; the head and neck, 9 percent; and the perineal region, 1 percent. The full-thickness burn involves the destruction of all epithelial elements and is characterized by a dry, pearly white or charred anesthetic surface. The degree of the body burned and the degree of full-thickness burn, as well as the number of days since the burn, must be considered (Seligman, 1974).

Every organ system is affected by a major burn. This results in important physiological and psychological imbalances in the child. If the burn is greater than 10 percent, the child is hospitalized (Raffensperger and Pokorny, 1974).

Emotional Reactions to Burns

The child is away from his home and separated from his family at this time. He is under great stress. He may not even be able to speak because of the stress of the physical restrictions of the medical apparatus. He may have all sorts of tubes occupying his body. Most of his energy is invested in surviving. It is important to be able to identify normal and pathological responses from the child, under the circumstances, to help prevent further psychological damage. Most children exhibit either a healthy response or a reactive disorder. Some have organic brain syndrome from cerebral edema. Pathological psychophysiologic disorders that the child might manifest include hypertension, ulcers, and a seizure like phenomenon. Normal mental mechanisms the child might exhibit include protesting (by yelling out), identification with the aggressor (the medical personnel), withdrawal to conserve energy to live, and denial. It must be ascertained that the child is withdrawing for life-conservation and not to die, because in the latter case, drastic measures would be necessary (Seligman, 1974).

Pain is a strong contributing factor in the psychological reactions of the burned child. His previous experience with pain is an important factor. Anxiety is a predominant effect, along with anger, submission, guilt, and depression. The child's reaction to pain can actually hinder his recovery. Pain can result in fear and panic in the child. In mild burns, pain can serve the useful purpose of aiding the child in active mastery or trauma and adaptation to the hospital. On the other hand, pain may lead to a feeling of profound helplessness. Pain and its accompanying anxiety represent a major event in the child's life and will be long remembered. The memory may result in the development of phobic defenses (Nover, 1973).

Long and Cope (1961) have done a most comprehensive study of the emotional problems of burned children. According to their study, the peculiar, distinctive behavior of burned children may be due to the following: (1) the trauma and immediate emotional threat, (2) hormonal and metabolic response, or (3) infection. The danger of the immediate trauma is the greatest problem. In some cases, the authors note, difficult behavior may have been present previous to the burn and is just continuing. The responses of hospital personnel to the child and his behavior and the reassurance to the parents and to the child from the parents can be crucial (Long and Cope, 1961).

The hospital environment and attitudes of staff members toward the care of the burned child play an important part in the atmosphere in the hospital and morale of all the personnel involved. Unsuccessful attempts by staff members to deal with the undesirable behavior manifested by the burned child can result in staff fatigue, feelings of helplessness, and frequent transfers of personnel (Shorkey and Taylor, 1973). The surgeon may be the primary medical person involved in a burn case, and yet, there is little in surgery literature about the emotional reactions of children (Nover, 1973). Burned children are particularly difficult to treat. They require especially kind and patient personnel and expensive space and equipment (Raffensperger and Pokorny, 1974). Communication with parents is especially important, and the parents' confidence and acceptance are communicated to the child; likewise, their fear and anxiety also come across. Medical personnel can help parents understand their child's reactions and, by understanding, modify them (Nover, 1973).

Amputations

Amputations during childhood are not frequent and result from a few, various, serious causes. Most amputations come as a result of failure to find another solution for serious infection or accident, for congenital anomalies, or for a cancerous condition. In pediatrics, an attempt is made to save all potentially useful tissue for use with prostheses. Because amputations are often complicated by subsequent overgrowth, they should only be carried out after long and careful consideration when no alternative procedure will suffice (Gellis and Kagan, 1968).

Prosthesis

Prosthetic devices are an immediate and essential consideration following amputation. Usually, prosthetic devices are supplied as the need for function emerges in the child's developmental pattern. The child's "gadget tolerance" varies and is an important factor. The level of the child's development is another essential element in selecting a prosthesis. The prosthesis chosen should be the simplest possible device to serve the purpose. An infant with an amputation at the wrist or below the elbow may be able to use a plastic mitten by three months of age and a movable hook by eighteen months. When the amputation is above the elbow, the hook and movable elbow are applied by twenty-four to thirty-six months. Children with lower-extremity amputation require simple prosthetic devices that allow them to pull to a standing position and to balance sometime between six and fifteen months, depending on their motor development. In the near future, prosthetic devices operated by external sources, such as batteries or motors, will be developed. Early fitting of prostheses is usually successful for the child when attention is paid to details. The device does require frequent checking to be sure it does not cause pain, is in good working order, and is the proper length and circumference (Gellis and Kagan, 1968).

Adjustment

There is evidence that children adjust more easily to artificial limbs than adults. In fact, a young person who may be very sensitive to deformity may welcome an amputation and replacement that can be covered with clothes and allows him to move normally without calling undue attention to itself. Rehabilitation of the amputee includes learning to perform the basic routines in living: maintaining personal hygiene and providing ambulation and transportation for himself (Clark and Cumley, 1973).

Legg-Calvé-Perthes Disease

Legg-Calvé-Perthes disease, sometimes known simply as Perthes disease or as osteochondrosis of the capital femoral epiphysis (Silver et al., 1973), is a common disorder of the hip affecting children between the ages of three and ten, with a peak incidence at age five. It affects boys much more often than girls (four to six times according to various researchers) (Jolly, 1968). This disease may have a gradual or sudden onset characterized by moderate pain in the hip, limitation of motion, and a progressively more intense limp in the involved leg (Magalini, 1971). Pain that is intermittent and not severe is the main diagnostic feature. The limp may be present, but not easy to detect. The loss of internal rotation of the hip joint is the most useful sign of the condition. The cause of the disease is thought to be avascular necrosis (Jolly, 1968), probably resulting from trauma to the hip, whether conspicuous or not. Absence of treatment may result in eventual atrophy of the muscles and shortening of the leg (Magalini, 1971). In some cases, the first symptoms may appear after a night's sleep. The symptoms may come and go during the years, resulting in the onset of crippling osteoarthritis in the third and fourth decades of life (Holt et al., 1962).

Treatment

Legg-Calvé-Perthes disease is a self-limiting condition that may persist for as long as two to four years. Early diagnosis and treatment are important; the main principle in management is to prevent permanent deformity (Gellis and Kagan, 1968). However, some eminent physicians say that treatment does not change the course of the disease or prevent later problems (Holt et al., 1962). Treatment may include prolonged immobilization with temporary use of traction (Jolly, 1968). Next, the use of a non-weight-bearing brace with a 3-inch buildup to the opposite shoe is begun and maintained until the condition is resolved. During this time, the child can remain with his family and friends and continue school attendance. The hip is examined for spasm and range-of-motion every six weeks, and x rays are taken and studies done every three months. During the two– to four-year course of the disease, the brace is lengthened frequently as the child grows. Every day, the child should do active muscle-setting exercises and active hip, knee, and ankle joint exercises to prevent muscle atrophy and joint limitation. When the hip has recovered, one to two months of protection with crutches is advisable. The opposite hip should be watched carefully, because bilateral osteochondrosis is not uncommon (Gellis and Kagan, 1968).

Prognosis

The prognosis with treatment of Legg-Calvé-Perthes disease usually is functional recovery. Of the patients, 30 percent have good recovery and 25 percent have continuous pain and limited movement, with others falling somewhere in between (Magalini, 1971). One difficulty in evaluating treatment is uncertainty in estimating the onset and the progress of the disease (Holt et al., 1962).

Medical personnel need to stress to patients and parents the importance of not bearing weight on the affected extremity for several months. It will be difficult for the active school child to undergo a period of prolonged immobility. Everyone in the child's environment should work together to find activities that keep the child occupied (Marlow, 1965).

Scoliosis

At all ages, the spine is normally straight, when viewed from the back. Variations take the form of an increase or decrease in normal curves or of the appearance of pathologic curves or protrusions (Holt et al., 1962). There are three abnormal curves. *Lordosis* is an inward curvature of the spine usually resulting from or associated with another disease. *Kyphosis* is a pronounced outward curvature of the spine sometimes referred to as *hump–* or *hunchback* (Clark and Crumley, 1973).

Scoliosis is the most serious spinal curvature. It is an S-shaped lateral curvature, usually associated with rotation of the spine. It is frequently seen in children between the ages of twelve and sixteen years, during the period of rapid growth. There are two basic types of scoliosis. One is correctable or functional scoliosis, usually caused by poor posture (Marlow, 1965). Postural scoliosis is often seen in girls ten to fifteen years old. When the child is asked to bend forward, the postural curve disappears, differentiating it from structural scoliosis. The condition is occasionally due to an inequality of leg length. It is not progressive and usually disappears with exercises (Jolly, 1968). It may be corrected by improving sitting habits and more rest, as well as general body fitness (Marlow, 1965).

Fixed or structural scoliosis may result from a congenital malformation of the vertebral column or associated malformations and is commonly acquired as a result of poliomyelitis or as a complication of another neuromuscular disease (Holt et al., 1962). The clinical manifestations occur during periods of spinal growth. There will probably be no pain until the later stages of the disease (Marlow, 1965). Early recognition is important to prevent an increase in the curvature. There may be associated shortness of breath because of diminished respiratory capacity or gastrointestinal upsets from the crowded abdominal organs (Latham and Heckel, 1967).

Diagnosis and Treatment

Diagnosis of scoliosis is made with a physical examination, including x rays of the patient in a standing position. Treatment includes a well-balanced diet high in animal protein and vitamins and minerals (Marlow, 1965). Other kinds of treatment depend on the nature of the curve and the rapidity of its progression. It is usually more deforming if it is a result of poliomyelitis, is secondary to structural anomalies, or has its onset early in life. Conservative treatment involves keeping the spine flexible with daily stretching exercises. A heel lift may be used to keep the pelvis level. Progress of the curve is followed by an x ray every three to six months. Progression of deformity or spinal rigidity are danger signals (Gellis and Kagan, 1968).

The spinal curvature may require surgical correction. Indications for surgery are rapid progression of the curve, the curve causing the child to stand out of balance, or the deformity being cosmetically objectionable (Gellis and Kagan, 1968). The spinal fusion would be performed when the child's growth is completed. Surgery would be followed by use of a cast and a brace worn to maintain the corrected position. The adolescent should be encouraged to maintain his usual interests and activities as much as possible (Latham and Heckel, 1967).

Multiple Sclerosis

Multiple sclerosis is not usually seen in children. It is likely, however, that the stage is set for the disease in the body sometime during childhood. Multiple sclerosis (MS) is a chronic disease that may have remission of symptoms, including weakness, muscular incoordination, jerking movements of the legs and arms, speech disturbance, and involuntary movement of the eyes (Clark and Cumley, 1973). It is prevalent in females and the onset, though difficult to identify, is usually between the ages of twenty and forty years. There are variable, multiple symptoms at the onset of the disease (Magalini, 1971). The first symptom may be a mistiness of vision that goes unnoticed. The patient may later experience double vision, a tingling sensation in his skin, lack of coordination, weakness, tremors, or stammering. The patient's speech may become monotonous or slurred. His leg muscles eventually become stiff and have spasms. Intelligence may deteriorate: Other mental symptoms may include depression and/or a state of euphoria. The most common emotional expression is a feeling of well-being resulting in a generally optimistic state of mind (Clark and Cumley, 1973).

Diagnosis and Prognosis

The diagnosis of multiple sclerosis may be difficult because the symptoms resemble those of many other disorders of the nervous system. No useful treatment is presently known. The patient is encouraged to stay in bed during acute attacks (Clark and Cumley, 1973). Symptomatic physiotherapy, good nutrition, and vitamins may be helpful (Magalini, 1971).

Causes of multiple sclerosis are unknown. Possibilities include toxic, viral, allergic, or metabolic reactions (Magalini, 1971). Some researchers in recent years have speculated that multiple sclerosis may result from an *autoimmunity* resulting when the body develops an allergy to part of itself. Multiple sclerosis develops early in the adult life of otherwise healthy people. The symptoms come and go over a period of years, in the long run usually resulting in complete disability (Clark and Cumley, 1973). However, years of well-being may follow each acute attack. There have been reports of a benign form with early arrest and a "clinically silent" form. The average survival is for ten to twenty years from the initial episode for other than benign cases. The later onset of the disease often results in a faster evolution and a shorter survival time (Magalini, 1971).

SENSORY DEFECTS
Friedreich's Ataxia

Friedreich's ataxia is an inherited disease in which there is a progressive degeneration of the sensory cells in the dorsal ganglia and nerves to the limbs and trunk. The condition usually has its onset in the first or second decade of life. One of the first signs is poor balance (ataxia), which results in frequent falling or a lurching, awkward gait. Later, the person becomes clumsy and "shaky." In school, the clumsiness interferes with physical education, and writing is impaired because of tremors of the upper extremities. Speech may become slurred, and the upper-extremity tremor often interferes with eating. There is a wasting away of the muscles of the limbs, and skeletal deformities appear in many of the persons. Spinal curvature appears in all but 20 percent of those in their teen-age lives.

Approximately 90 percent of the people with Friedreich's ataxia (FA) manifest heart abnormalities. A large percentage of individuals suffering from FA have eye problems, including optic nerve atrophy.

FA is a rare disease, but the familial incidence is common, because the disease may be inherited through a recessive gene. This means, of course, that both parents must contribute a defective gene, or it can be transmitted in an autosomal dominant way in which one affected parent or affected siblings are the rule.

Children suffering from FA should remain in the regular classroom as long as possible. Later, the child may have to go to a special class or school. If mental retardation is not involved, the child should be treated educationally like other children.

Later, the FA child may need physical therapy that regular schools cannot provide. The child may also have seizures controllable by medication. In any case, the regular classroom is the place for this child, as long as the child's condition is tolerant.

Visual Impairments

The American Foundation for the Blind, Inc. (1976) indicates that severe visual impairment may be called *blindness* or *functional* or *legal* blindness. A person is said to be legally blind if his central visual acuity does not exceed 20/200 in the better eye with corrective lenses or his visual field is less than an angle of twenty degrees. A person is considered "legally blind" if s/he can see no further than someone with normal sight can see at the distance of 200 feet. Functional blindness is the inability to read newspaper print, and legal blindness is a definition to determine eligibility for public assistance.

There are many definitions of blindness: They all refer to how well the individual can see with the best corrective lenses. Actually, 75 percent of all blind people have some usable vision.

In deciding when a person should be considered severely visually impaired, the primary concern should be how well the person can function with his limited vision.

It is estimated that there are about 6.4 million people in the United States with some kind of visual impairment. These are people who have trouble seeing even with corrective lenses. Of these, 1.7 million are severely impaired, which means that they are either legally blind or that they function as if they were legally blind, even though their vision may not fall into that definition. Only about 400,000 of the severely visually impaired have no usable vision at all.

Over 1 million persons or about 65 percent of the severely visually impaired are sixty-five years of age or older. This is because the diseases that are the major causes of blindness in this country are associated primarily with aging. This is also the result of an increased life expectancy. About 20,000 persons or 12 percent of the severely visually impaired are in the labor force. There are approximately 60,000 severely visually impaired children of school or preschool age in the United States. About 40,000 of these are in school, including an estimated 3,000 college students, and 20,000 are still too young to be in a school situation. These children make up about 3 percent of the severely visually impaired population.

Causes

A large number of the partially sighted are affected by prenatal conditions, some of which are hereditary. Other causes may be diseases, accidents, or developmental anomalies (Table I).

Table I.
CAUSES OF BLINDNESS

Heredity	15%
Infectious diseases	7%
Prenatal causes	50%
Injuries	3%
Poisoning	20%
Tumors	5%
	100%

The Blind

Only about 20 percent of all legally blind children and adults are totally blind; therefore, for the purpose of this chapter, the child with a visual acuity of 20/200 or less in the better eye after correction is discussed. After 20/200 on the continuum would be *counts fingers,* followed by *hand movement,* and *light perception* and *projection.*

Characteristics

Myers (1930) found that, out of 2860 blind children, 50.2 percent were boys, and 49.8 percent were girls. It should be mentioned in this chapter that mental retardation is not a necessary concomitant of blindness. Many available studies indicate that partially seeing children do not deviate to any great extent from seeing children as far as intelligence is concerned.

There is much controversy concerning the emotional adjustment of the blind and the partially seeing. Meyerson (1953) has pointed out the many discrepancies in the research concerning the adjustment of this group. Cowen (1961), in one of the most sophisticated studies, found no great difference between the blind in residential schools, the blind in day schools, and a group of seeing students in comparable situations.

Education

The education of the blind and partially sighted, as with all persons, begins at birth and continues throughout life. The visually handicapped person has special educational needs the sighted person does not have. These needs are met in varying ways. How these needs are fulfilled and how well they are fulfilled depends upon the degree of disability, the facilities available to the person, and upon the person himself.

The visually-handicapped child begins life with the basic needs of any child. Jones (1963) states, "The child who is handicapped by a visual loss or impairment must have the love and care of his parents just like his normally seeing brothers and sisters. He may have even greater need for their attention if he is to make a healthy adjustment to his defect."

Given a comfortable environment, a child whose only handicap is visual should acquire many skills at about the same age as a fully sighted child. He should learn to walk, talk, develop independent eating habits, and be toilet trained at about the same age as his sighted counterpart.

A blind or partially sighted and otherwise normal child can be taught in pre– and early school years to acquire educational aids, such as nonvisual cues. The following are nonvisual cues: smells, sounds, textures, air pockets, and tastes.

A bakery with its characteristic aroma serves to locate it as a landmark or informs the blind person of its purpose. An automobile has a sound all of its own. This sound identifies the street as a major thoroughfare or points out the location of a possible means of transportation. The wind can give a great deal of information: It rustles through the leaves and sighs through pine branches. If constant, it can give a method of checking one's direction. If a person steps past the protection of a building, its unchecked gust identifies an open space adjacent to him. A driveway can act as a landmark and can be distinguished as a break in the sidewalk, or a gravel strip through concrete. These and similar aids can greatly increase a blind child's orientation and mobility.

If possible, a blind or partially-seeing child should have nursery school experience with seeing children. Pauline Moore (1952), in her still-relevant study done twenty-five years ago, found that the teacher of seeing children usually required some reassurance before accepting a blind or partially sighted child into his/her class. The teacher usually had fears concerning the child's safety, the adequacy of the size of the staff, and concern for the common good of the group. Certain standards of readiness were adopted, and most of the children in this study met them between three and one-half and five years of age. These standards were not too difficult from those set for seeing children. However, the children with visual disabilities were usually placed in a group of younger children. Moore concluded that the experiences of the children she followed were most worthwhile: "The independence stressed in a nursery school program was extremely important to all the blind children in helping them to develop initiative and to build confidence in themselves." She also found some carry–over of learning from school to home and the development of many positive attitudes for all the children.

The Hearing-Impaired Child

The partially hearing child has always been a member of the regular classroom or was placed in an institution. Until the development of the pure tone audiometer and the hearing aid, however, he was usually classified as a troublemaker, because of his inability to hear the teacher or the recitation of his classmates.

Recently there has been a spurt of interest and a positive movement begun toward better education for the deaf and hard of hearing.

Love (1976) describes the partially hearing as those for whom the loss of hearing is educationally significant, but whose residual hearing is sufficient for interpreting speech with or without the use of a hearing aid. The educationally hard-of-hearing possess hearing levels of 30 to 59 decibels or a little higher.

Hearing loss refers to all degrees of hearing beyond 15 dB. (The decibel [dB] is a unit of measure used to express the magnitude of sound power or sound pressure.) The deaf have a hearing loss that is very severe, and the use of residual hearing is nonfunctional for discrimination of speech.

Early Education

The early education of the deaf child is very important. Of the children currently enrolled in schools for the deaf in the United States, 10 percent are under six years of age. The private and residential schools for the deaf also have a large number of preschool children enrolled.

Most deaf children are deaf from birth or before they have developed speech sufficiently to have obtained a permanent mastery of it, i.e. before preschool age. About two fifths of all deafness is congenital, and the remainder is accounted for by diseases and accidents, but more often by diseases. The diseases primarily responsible are meningitis, scarlet fever, measles, whooping cough, and abcesses of the ear and head.

Most parents have a difficult time accepting the fact that they have a deaf child and tend to hope that the child is just slow in developing. But because the infant cannot hear, he becomes handicapped very early; this handicapping process starts at the age of about three months. Naturally, infants receive enjoyment from vocalizing. Normal babies have started babbling by the age of six months. The deaf child babbles, too, and his tones and sounds are very much like those of a normal child. If one did not know, it would be impossible to tell the differences between the two. However, the deaf child is not imitating the voices of others; he is merely engaging in chance vocalizations. Ewing (1958) states that at about the ninth month, the hearing child will probably look up when he hears his name and also responds to a few other words. It is here that the deaf child really begins to fall behind in his development. The hearing child begins to understand words and obey them, but the deaf child can only imitate gestures.

A deaf child's parents need not wait until the child fails to talk to discover that he is deaf. There are many other ways to discover this: The parents can talk or make noises at different distances behind the child to see if he responds. If they suspect that the child has impaired hearing, they should take him to an otologist, a medical doctor specializing in ear problems. The otologist can test the child for hearing loss as early as seven months of age. It is stated by Ewing (1958) that, of severely deaf children, most drag their feet and are very clumsy, and they tend to sit up and walk later than ordinary children.

When parents discover they have a deaf child, they must accept the fact that the child is to be treated as much like a normal child as possible. Perhaps the only benefit of the parents not discovering the child's deafness at an early age is that they treat the child as normal when they think that s/he is normal. The more normally the child is treated, the better adjusted s/he and his/her family will be. It is difficult for the parents to accept the fact that only in very few cases can the child's deficiency be cured.

Special procedures have been developed to teach deaf children to speak, using the senses of touch, sight, and sound; usually, the child is two years old before s/he can be admitted to special schools. As soon as a parent discovers that his baby is deaf, s/he should immediately find out what can be done to help. Usually, the parents can do a great deal to prepare the child for education, and, in some cities, the schools for the deaf provide two-week courses for the parents of deaf children. If the parents do not live near such a school, home courses are available. Most parents need to overteach their children and forget that all the learning must take place in normal family-like situations. The teaching should be fun, and the desire to communicate must be promoted. One of the best things that a parent can do is talk to child in a pleasant tone using animated facial expressions.

The otologist can discover whether the child has residual hearing. If s/he has, a hearing aid should be obtained as soon as possible, and the child should be taught how to use it to the fullest advantage. Frampton and Gall (1955) say that when talking to a deaf child, a person should always get the child's attention and then talk directly facing him. The more the child is spoken to, the more he will want to respond in speech. Deaf children are more dependent upon their parents than hearing children, and because of this, the parents have extra responsibilities.

Preschool Education

Most authorities believe that if the deaf child learns to speak by parental training, he should be placed in an ordinary nursery or kindergarten. If he does not, he should be placed in a special nursery or day school for deaf children as soon as possible. By the time a deaf child finishes one of these schools, according to Ewing and Ewing (1958), he should be able to enter an elementary school at about the same level of development as that of a hearing child. If the parents live in a rural district or small town, the child should be sent to a residential or boarding school for the deaf.

Many authorities believe the main aim of education for the

deaf child is to give him words to think with, to understand the expressed thoughts of others, and to enable him to express his thoughts. The child should be reached very early and, during these impressionable years, must have his/her beginnings in communications established. Therefore, s/he should be admitted to school at the earliest possible age.

In nurseries, deaf children have routines similar to normal children, except that special emphasis is placed on lipreading. After the child becomes familiar with the activities of the school, it becomes easy for him to recognize that certain movements of the teacher's lips must mean "Take off your coat," or "We're going out to play," because these are the things that have always happened at this time of the day. Thus, the beginning of the child's lipreading occurs. Now, with residual hearing, a hearing aid may be introduced. At first, the child should wear it just a few minutes each day in order to hear a sound.

Chronic Illness

Traumatic physical conditions in children may involve either chronic or acute syndromes. Each presents its own special challenge. There are several common problems in chronic illness. Chronic illness leads to particular kinds of psychological consequences that must be dealt with. The attitudes of society toward the disease and children with it may be detrimental. The family with the child with a serious chronic illness may need financial help for the duration, and money is needed for medical research providing more information about the disease. Many of these factors depend heavily on the strength of the national organization. Often the use of specialists for the child with a chronic illness makes it unclear which medical person provides guidance to the patient and his family. One important goal for the physician and other people around the patient is to prevent secondary personality handicaps. The physician needs to assume a larger and more personal role in the care of the chronically ill child. The physician's training and his guidance to the child and his family should consider the chronic illness in the context of the family and the community (Pless, 1973).

Emergency Care In Acute Problems

Emergency care for acute problems provides a different demand for medical services. One half of all deaths of children come as a result of accidents. The crippling injuries and rehabilitation make an even greater impact on society than would the child's death. The problem of trauma resulting from accidents should be brought into sharp public focus, in order to enlist local and national support for studies in accident prevention and the management of major injuries resulting from trauma caused by accidents (Haller, 1973).

During the immediate aftermath of an acute trauma, the child may have temporarily lost the ability to communicate precisely. Therefore, an evaluation of his physical condition will demand great insight and patience on the part of attending medical personnel. The physican needs to be able to establish a meaningful relationship with the child. Much will depend on an objective evaluation of the child's condition, with no reliance on communication from the child.

Child's Emotional Well-Being

Emergency trauma can have particularly disastrous effects on the child's emotional well-being. The terror caused by separation from his family at this time under these circumstances may result in serious emotional after effects. Emergency rooms need to be prepared to provide protective care to the injured child. A special trauma center for children might include novel techniques for transporting the injured child, a resuscitation area, core diagnostic facilities, and staff knowledgeable and experienced in providing the special kind of care needed. An intensive care area especially for children and available operating rooms would need to be a part of the total plant.

The backbone of successful therapy in children is rapid evaluation and speedy sequential correction of altered physiology. The child's unique metabolic demands and his miniature anatomic relationships provide a special challenge to the physician. The rewards for the successful management of traumas occurring in childhood are great. The younger the child when he is injured, the more valuable is society's investment in his future (Haller, 1973).

The Pediatrician's Role

The pediatrician plays an important role in child health care. He is often the primary medical person involved. In his/her practice, statistics show that s/he may see two neonatal and one other death per year, so the dying child will not be a large part of his practice, but 10 percent of the children he sees will have some kind of chronic disorder. Of his practice, 50 percent is involved in well-child care. It may be time for the practice of pediatrics to be moving in new directions. Pediatricians may need to be more concerned with morbidity and chronic problems. There should be greater emphasis on prevention of disease and of accidents and on early crisis intervention. The use of *neighborhood health centers* might be one way to promote health maintenance (Haggerty, 1974). The surgeon may plan an important role in the care of children involved in trauma. Surgery literature might include cognizance of the emotional implications of surgery for children (Nover, 1973).

Nurses and emergency room personnel need special training in the care of children with traumatic conditions. Perhaps special kinds of people are needed to provide these services. Inadequate care of the child can lead to a decrease in general staff morale, as well as to bad times for the child (Shorkey and Taylor, 1973). In any case of prolonged medical care for a child, there should be a systematic provision of someone to provide supervision for the case and medical guidance for the child and his family.

Care for the Child in Pain

Shorkey and Taylor (1973) discuss the possible use of behavior modification with children in great pain. At the time the child is experiencing the pain, s/he is unable to achieve his customary positive reinforcement. He may in fact learn avoidance or escape behaviors. Any aspect of treatment may by association become the source of great pain and/or anxiety. There may be little relief from aversive influences. The child may regress to behavior that resulted in positive reinforcement at an earlier time in his life. Frustration, aggression, or depression may also result from the interference of pain with the child's ability to gain positive reinforcement. Behavior modification techniques may be helpful in counteracting these negative responses to pain. Decisions to use this technique need to be made on an individual-case basis.

Whenever possible, the sick child might be cared for at home to prevent the emotional trauma of separation from home and family. Taking care of their own child can be a good experience for parents. They have helped him recover, and they become more competent and increase their confidence in their abilities as parents. It is useful for the parents to know the techniques involved in caring for their child. They should, however, be encouraged to maintain their parental roles during the child's illness and not take on the role of doctor (Jolly, 1968).

If hospitalization is necessary, steps can be taken to alleviate anxiety associated with a hospital stay, especially if it is known about ahead of time. The child can be prepared in advance for his hospital stay. His parents can stay as close as possible, rooming in, when this is available. Playrooms for convalescing children can be extremely valuable, and allowing the child to have familiar toys and blankets in the hospital can also help. Visiting hours should be as liberal as feasible: A parent should be present when the child is experiencing a crisis, returning to consciousness, for example. A supervised recreational program can be useful to the recuperating child. For children with long-term illness, care should be individualized, family-centered, and utilizing as many community resources as practical (Hamilton, 1970). During prolonged hospitalization, there may be a teacher in the hospital setting. S/He can check with the child's regular school to help the child stay in touch with the education process and keep up with his lessons (Jolly, 1968).

Parental Reactions to Childhood Illness

Parents may have a very difficult time facing their sick child. They may feel guilty about hostility they have felt and they may feel they gave the child inadequate care, which might have caused the illness or accident. They may feel very little confidence in their own ability to take care of their child. Parents may need support for themselves during this time of medical crisis for their child. They need reassurance from the medical staff, and they need to be aware of what is happening to their child from the inside, as well as from the outside. There is evidence that a positive response in parents results in less stress for the child. Sometimes a special group for parents can help them deal with issues. There can be very constructive interaction among parents who may be having some of the same experiences. Parents can help each other handle their fears and gain support from each other. Such an experience can increase the parents' awareness of appropriate ways to handle the hospital experience. The parents' groups can make the hospital more aware of and responsive to the needs of parents and children (Irwin and Lloyd, 1974).

Usually, the child who has had a favorable hospital experience and returns home in good health adjusts rapidly to life at home, especially if his home is happy and he feels loved. The most important factors for the child returning home from the hospital are the medical state of his health and the psychological and material nature of his home. Long hospitalization may be traumatic to the parent and the child. Other family members may have been neglected. The parents need confidence that they can again establish and maintain supervision over the child and his health. With reassurance from the hospital personnel and encouragement and careful instruction from the doctor, the parent should be able to take care of the child adequately, and family life should return to normal.

REFERENCES

American Foundation for the Blind, Inc.: *Facts About Blindness.* New York, American Foundation for the Blind, Inc., 1975.

Clark, R.L. and Cumley, R.W.: *The Book of Health.* New York, Van Nostrand Reinhold, 1973.

Cowen, E.F. et. al.: *Adjustment to Visual Disability in Adolescence.* New York, American Foundation for the Blind, Inc., 1961.

Ewing, I.R. and Ewing, A.W.G.: *New Opportunities for Deaf Children.* Springfield, Thomas, 1958.

Frampton, M.E. and Gall, E.D.: *Special Education for the Exceptional.* Boston, Sargent, 1955, vol. 1.

Gellis, S.S. and Kagan, B.M.: *Current Pediatric Therapy.* Philadelphia, Saunders, 1968.

Haggerty, R.J.: The changing role of the pediatrician in child health care. *Am J Dis Child, 127*:545-549, 1974.

Haller, J.A.: Newer concepts in emergency care of children with major injuries. *Md State Med J, 22*:65-68, 1973.

Hamilton, P.M.: *Basic Pediatric Nursing.* St. Louis, Mosby, 1970.

Holt, L.E., McIntosh, R., and Barnett, H.L.: *Pediatrics.* New York, Appleton, 1962.

Ilg, F.L. and Ames, L.R.: *Child Behavior.* New York, Dell, 1964.

Irwin, S. and Lloyd-Still, D.: The use of groups to mobilize parental strength during hospitalization of children. *Child Welfare, 53*:305-312, 1974.

Jolly, H.: *Diseases of Children.* Oxford, England, Blackwell Scientific Publications, 1968.

Jones, J.W.: *The Visually Handicapped Child.* U.S. Department of Health, Education and Welfare, Bulletin No. 39, 1963.

Latham, H.C., and Heckel, R.V.: *Pediatric Nursing.* St. Louis, Mosby, 1967.

Long, R.T. and Cope, O.: *Emotional Problems of Burned Children. N Engl J Med, 264*:1121-1127, 1961.

Love, H.D.: *A Handbook of Medical, Educational, and Psychological Information for Teachers of Physically Handicapped Children.* Springfield, Thomas, 1976.

Magalini, S.: *Dictionary of Medical Syndromes.* Philadelphia, Lippincott, 1971.

Marlow, D.R.: *Textbook of Pediatric Nursing.* Philadelphia, Saunders, 1965.

Meyerson, L.: The visually handicapped. *Review Educ Res, 23*:65, 1953.

Moore, P.M.: *A Blind Child, Too, Can Go to Nursery School.* American Foundation for the Blind, Pre-School Series No. 1, 1952.

Myers, E.T.: A survey of sight-saving classes in the public schools of the United States. *The Sight-Saving Class Exchange.* New York, National Society for the Prevention of Blindness, 1930.

Nover, R.A.: Pain and the burned child. *J Am Acad Child Psychiatry, 12*: 499-505, 1973.

Petrillo, M. and Sanger, S.: *Emotional Care of Hospitalized Children.* Philadelphia, Lippincott, 1972.

Pless, J.B.: The challenge of chronic illness. *Am J Dis Child, 126*:741-742, 1973.

Raffensperger, J.G., and Pokorny, W.J.: Treatment of children with burns. *Ill Med J, 145*:352-355, 1974.

Randolph, J., Tunell, W.P., and Lilly, J.R.: Thermal burns in children. *Med Ann DC, 43*:341-347, 1974.

Seligman, R.: A physciatric classification system for burned children. *Am J Psychiatry, 131*:41-46, 1974.

Shorkley, C.T. and Taylor, J.E.: Management of maladaptive behavior of a severely burned child. *Child Welfare, 52*:543-545, 1973.

Silver, H.K., Kempe, C.H., and Bruyn, H.B.: *Handbook of Pediatrics.* Los Altos, California, Lange, 1973.

Webster's New Twentieth Century Dictionary of the English Language, Cleveland. *World Pub,* 1959.

Chapter 2

OVERVIEW OF SPECIAL HEALTH PROBLEMS

CHILDREN with special health problems are those whose weakened physical condition renders them relatively inactive or slow or requires special precautions. *Low vitality* was used quite often in previous years to refer to a child with a chronic or special health problem.

Children with special health problems more often than not have at least normal intelligence and should be treated and taught like normal children. If at all possible, these children with low vitality should be placed in the regular classroom; they must be kept in the mainstream and not segregated. The teacher must look at the child's educational needs, just as s/he should any normal child's in the class. S/he should not place a cloud or shell around this child, and s/he has to have faith in the child.

Parental Attitudes

In the search for information pertaining to parental attitudes toward these children with chronic diseases, etc., five reactions of parents were found to be more common than others. These were (1) anxiety, (2) disbelief, (3) hostility, (4) helplessness, and (5) resentment.

A serious threat occurs to the set of values an individual establishes as a parent when a child in the family is sick for a long period of time. The dismay, the fear of the unknown concerning the condition in the child's future, and the feeling of helplessness combine to make the burden great. Other parents cannot bring themselves to face the reality of this type of handicap. They try to keep the neighbors from knowing; they may neglect to seek the help they need; or they may go from one doctor to another refusing to believe the diagnosis. Many times, they are really trying to find someone who will tell them that it is not as bad as they fear.

The term *special health problems* encompasses a multiplicity of conditions.   Cardiac conditions, spina bifida, malnutrition, epilepsy, diabetes, allergic disorders, anemia, tuberculosis, various crippling conditions, and leukemia are some of them.   The common elements in all of these conditions include chronic illness, the need for continuing medical attention, and certain restrictions of activity necessarily imposed on the individual.

Although research has been conducted on specific special health problems, there is little in the literature concerning the general topic of parental attitudes toward children with special health problems.   The available material deals with the more general topic of parental attitudes toward handicapped children. Parental attitudes toward all types of handicaps do not seem to be influenced by the causative factors or the severity of the handicap as much as by the general adjustment of the parents: The better adjusted the parent, the better able he is to cope with the handicap of the child.

When considering parental reactions to a special health problem, it is important to remember that in some instances these health problems develop after the child has lived a normal life for some period of time.   Many of these children are normal at birth and their problem develops later.   In some cases the condition is apparent or at least suspected during infancy.

Sickle Cell Anemia

Sickle cell anemia was first described several years ago by Dr. James E. Herrick after his evaluation of a young Negro boy who had a mysterious blood disease.   Doctor Herrick noted that the boy's blood cells had an unusual shape, and the term *sickle cell* was coined to describe this unusual shape or the changes in the shape.   The cells change from the flat biconcave disk of normal red blood cells to a long, thin, angular red cell reminiscent of grain-cutting sickles.

The sickled red cells are removed by the body in a very rapid rate, because the body recognizes their abnormal shape, and through a natural process, destroys these abnormal cells. Therefore, there is a rapid destruction of hemoglobin, which causes a jaundice of the whites of the eyes. The bone marrow, in turn, manufactures large numbers of new red cells, while trying to compensate for the anemia. Most people with sickle cell disease will have only one-half or one-third as many red cells as the normal individual. The sickled red cells are very rigid; therefore, it is not easy for them to pass through small blood vessels. They tend to "jam up" and while doing this, deprive tissue of the proper blood flow. This is called *vaso-occlusive episode*. When this happens, the tissues are bereft of their normal oxygen supply, and it causes great pain to the patient and sometimes, death.

When a child under the age of three has sickle cell anemia, the disease usually involves the bones of the hands and feet. This results in swelling and in painful extremities. The bones may even become fragile and weak because of the jam of the blood flow.

The vaso-occlusion phenomenon can also occur in the intestines, and when it does, the child will have severe stomach pain and cramping. The pain can be so severe that the child doubles over, and in many cases, the stomach becomes distended and tender to the touch. In many children, the spleen is affected, and the filtering out of abnormally shaped red blood cells is impaired. This could cause blood clots and, following these clots, severe pain will occur. Also, the child's liver can be affected, and this can be very serious and often requires hospitalization and treatment.

Liver involvement usually causes jaundice and distended abdomen, nausea, and a tremendous loss of appetite. The child can also have gall bladder problems, because when the red blood cells are broken down, bilirubin is formed as a waste product. The bilirubin and bile salts are removed from the blood by the liver. As the rate of red blood cells breakdown increases, the bilirubin and blood salt formation increases. Because of the increased amount of bile formation, gall bladder stones are very common. Gall stones can be extremely severe and often result in the surgical removal of the gall bladder and the stones.

The child having sickle cell anemia will have to have an adjusted schedule in school where he will not participate in activities that require vigorous exercise. The school nurse must also watch him carefully and notify parents of any of the symptoms that would cause discomfort and pain. The child will not be affected academically, because this condition has nothing to do with the destruction of brain cells; therefore, his academic regimen would be the same as for the child not affected by sickle cell disease.

Hemophilia

The word *hemophilia* is used to describe a hereditary condition in which the blood clots very slowly or not at all. Therefore, a cut or abrasion could cause excessive blood loss and even death. Generally, this condition affects males and is transmitted by females.

There are so many bleeding disorders associated with vascular and platelet abnormalities that they could not all be covered in the scope of this chapter. Therefore, only two deficiencies will be described. These conditions are called factor VIII and factor IX and are transmitted as sex-linked recessive factors. This means, of course, that the abnormal factor is carried by the female who has a 50 percent chance of passing the abnormality off to her male child. If the male offspring inherits the condition from his mother, he will thus have *hemophilia.* The female carrier also has a 50 percent chance of transmitting the disorder to her female child, but if the female child inherits the disorder from her mother, she does not have the condition known as hemophilia, but is a carrier.

A male affected by hemophilia transmits the disorder to all his female offspring, and all of his girl children will be carriers. A male, though, who is a hemophiliac, will not transmit the abnormality to any of his sons. Males, therefore, must inherit hemophilia from their mothers, or in some cases, develop hemophilia as a new disease in the family.

Platelets

Platelets are small bodies that float in the blood and adhere to any tissue, except the lining of the normal blood vessel. These platelets plug the opening when a blood vessel is broken and, thereby, prevent blood loss. They also release chemical mediators that cause the smooth muscles close to the blood vessels to contract, attracting more platelets to the area, and they also release enzymes that aid in formation of clotting. Platelet abnormalities are found in hemophiliacs; therefore, the clotting process, when the vessel is injured, is impaired.

Treatment and Prognosis

During the last several years, there have been two major medical developments that have greatly aided in the care and prognosis of children having hemophilia. Factor concentrates are now readily available to replace the deficient factors VIII and IX, and parents and patients can be taught home administration of these concentrates to provide immediate treatment if bleeding is suspected.

People with hemophilia must have limited activity. The school should have knowledge of the condition, and the child should not engage in sports that would involve the danger of bruising or cutting. It should be remembered, however, that a child with hemophilia cannot be deprived of social and physical needs, or he will suffer a grave injustice.

Congenital Heart Disease

Congenital (at birth) heart disease is much more common in childhood than acquired heart disease: It is twenty times more common than the acquired. Concerning the incidence of congenital heart disease, the best information states 6 children are born with this condition for every 1000 live births. The reader will notice live births were mentioned, because if still births were included, the incidence would be much higher. Studies of ten-year-old children who had been untreated because of congenital heart disease found that there is about 1 or 2 per 1000. The main reason for the difference between those born and ten-year-olds is that the attrition is largely the result of death from the more serious congenital heart diseases. The largest number of children die the first year after birth.

Etiology (Causes)

In the fetus, the basic development of the heart takes place at a very early stage. The fetus' heart begins to take a recognizable shape toward the end of the third intrauterine week. The heart begins as a tube and a combination of differential growth. The major cardiovascular structure is formed by the end of the seventh week. Consequently, the severe abnormalities of cardiovascular structure found in the fetus occurs before the eighth week.

Environmental influences during the pregnancy, such as drugs and viruses, etc., have been implicated in the cause of congenital heart disease. Chromosomal abnormalities and single mutant gene syndromes have also been implicated in the etiology of this disease. An important finding from research is that pregnant women who contract German measles within the first three months of pregnancy are prone to giving birth to children with abnormalities of the heart and vessels.

Diagnosis

There are many clues that parents should look for that would make them suspect that their child has cardiovascular disease. The most common complaints by the child are fatigue, shortness of breath, chest pain, cyanosis (blueness of the lips and nail beds), fainting, and poor growth and chest development.

The family physician often discovers a heart murmur when the child is being examined routinely or for childhood diseases. The heart murmur is an abnormal heart sound, but it definitely does not always signify heart disease. After the physician discovers an abnormal sound or suspects abnormality, he may prescribe further tests that could include cardiac catheterization and angiocardiography.

The process of cardiac catheterization takes place in the hopsital. A thin plastic tube is inserted into the appropriate vessel in the person's arm or leg and advanced through the vessel into the heart chambers and related arteries or veins. With fluoroscopic guidance, the nature of the defect is determined medically by measuring oxygen saturation of blood samples taken from the heart chambers and associated vessels. In angiography, a radio-paque fluid is injected into the blood vessel or heart chambers, and x rays of the heart are taken. The physician can see structural malformations of the heart through this process.

Educational Implications

Each child has a different condition that affects him differently; therefore, it is impossible to give limitations for each child who has a heart problem. However, it can be stated accurately that a child with a heart condition should not engage in competitive athletics unless he has specific approval of a physician.

The teacher and school nurse should be alerted to the child's condition so they can watch for any signs of trouble. The teacher should watch for shortness of breath, chest pain, faintness, cyanosis, very rapid heart beat, and unusual fatigue. The child should be encouraged and counseled to a vocation which does not require physical labor.

The child with a specific heart condition should be educated in the regular classroom and have only a few things different from the normal child. There is the possibility that he can be given the services of a resource room if one is available, but only if he has academic problems not related to his physical condition.

Leukemias

Acute Leukemias

The acute leukemias are characterized by an increase in very immature leukocytes. These leukocytes are usually myelo– or lymphoblasts, which are found in the blood and/or bone marrow. The lympho– and myeloblastic forms differ in their response to therapy, age distribution, and in many other ways, but also, there is a considerable similarity in their modes of presentation and complications. Acute leukemia can occur in persons of any age from the prenatal to age 100.

Acute Lymphoblastic Leukemia

It is true that acute lymphoblastic leukemia can occur at any age, but it should be pointed out that it is predominantly found in children. In this acute type, the leukemic cell is quite immature and typically has a fine nuclear chromatin nucleoli.

Definition

Leukemia is the generalized proliferation of the blood-forming tissues, usually involving the leukocyte series. An oversimplified statement is the white blood cells become too numerous in the blood stream due to a disease of the bone marrow, which is probably cancerous. According to the type of corpuscles present, the disease may be called (1) *lymphatic* or (2) *myeloid* leukemia. In lymphatic leukemia, the spleen and lymph glands are affected, and in myeloid, the ribs, sternum, vertabrae, and bone marrow are affected.

Incidence

It can be stated with a great deal of accuracy that acute lymphatic leukemia is repeatedly fatal; the average untreated patient survives about four to six months from the onset of the disease. The fact that the victim of acute leukemia will live only a short time is already stated; therefore, his educational implications must of necessity be short-term. Other than medication and rest periods at the onset of the disease, the child can perform normally in the classroom with no special equipment. As the disease progresses, the child will have to be placed under the direction of a private tutor, or if confined to a hospital, the teacher is provided by the hospital.

Etiology

Some forms of leukemia in chickens, mice, and rats are due to viruses, and there is increasing evidence that viruses cause similar forms of leukemia in man. Although there are many definitions of leukemia, presently, for the discussion in this book, it may be regarded as a cancer of the blood-forming organisms. It appears that genetic factors are not conspicuous in the occurrence of leukemia in man. In many cases, however, exposure to environmental factors, such as x rays, radioactive materials, and certain chemicals may be associated with the disease.

Symptoms

The person suffering from leukemia often feels weak, fatigues quite easily, has a white complexion, and generally has a gradual or acute weight loss. Often, this person has moderate anemia and sometimes runs a low-grade fever. Very often the spleen enlarges, which is a frequent cause of discomfort, and the person may also complain of bone pain and also have skin lesions. In the early stages of the disease, bleeding tendencies are rare, but in the advanced stage, spontaneous hemorrhaging often occurs.

Treatment

The person having leukemia is often treated with steroids and other drugs, such as the folic acid antagonists, which have generally temporary beneficial effects. Frequently, blood transfusions may be necessary and, in the case of chronic leukemia, treatment consists of irradiation with x rays or the administration of radioactive substances, such as radiophosphorous and a variety of chemical substances having in common the ability to suppress the abnormal growth of cells.

Cystic Fibrosis

Cystic fibrosis is a congenital, inherited disease affecting the pancreas, respiratory system, and sweat glands. It usually begins in infancy and is typified by chronic respiratory infection, pancreatic insufficiency, and susceptibility to heat prostation. This condition is the leading cause of chronic lung disease in American babies and affects about 1 out of every 800. Caucasians are the primary race suffering cystic fibrosis, and it occurs in a few American Negroes. However, it is a very rare occurrence in Orientals. Through the National Cystic Fibrosis Foundation in New York, greater numbers of people are becoming aware of this disease.

Cystic fibrosis may occur in either sex, and it is inherited from both sides of the family. If only one parent carries the gene for cystic fibrosis, that parent will have no symptoms. If he has children, there will be a fifty-fifty chance that these children will be carriers of the recessive gene, but none will have the disease or any of the symptoms. However, if both parents carry the gene, each child will have a one-in-four chance of having cystic fibrosis. Not many years ago, cystic fibrosis was confined to infancy and early childhood because the disease resulted in early death. Now, these individuals often live to thirty-five or forty years of age and even older. They often function as normal human beings and have children who do not have the disease.

It is believed that in the United States there are over 10 million people who carry the recessive gene for cystic fibrosis. The odds are twenty to one that any one person is a carrier of the gene. People can have tests made to detect if they are carriers.

It was not long ago that cystic fibrosis was considered a rare but fatal disease. Now it is recognized as a very common disease, and it is known that patients can lead a rewarding life, if the condition is discovered early.

Almost all of the exocrine glands of an individual with cystic fibrosis are affected to some degree of severity. In all cases, the sweat of the diseased person has a high level of salt. Because of this high salt content, large amounts of salt are lost from the body.

The main sources of complications are the mucous glands. These secrete abnormally thick, gluey mucus. In a normal adult, the mucus is thin and slippery, and it keeps air passages clear by carrying off dust particles and germs. In a person suffering from cystic fibrosis, the air passages become clogged because of the thick mucus. It is possible that his/her digestion, lungs, and liver may also be affected.

Educational Implications

The child with cystic fibrosis is under the care of a physician. The teacher must be aware that the child does not have a communicable disease also that his energy level is not as high as that of other children. Therefore, he will fatigue easier than the other children. Knowing these things, the teacher in the regular classroom can help the child carry on a fairly normal existence. The teacher will also need to work very closely with the child's parents to know of any changes in the child's condition and also to help the parents teach the child at home during convalescence.

Because of the tremendous scientific strides that have been made concerning the control of cystic fibrosis, most children having this disease can be educated in the regular classroom, assuming they do not have other handicapping conditions. These children miss school more than the average, and possibly, a homebound teacher is consulted periodically.

One big problem that the teacher faces will be the peer disapproval of the child with cystic fibrosis. The teacher must ever strive to insure that the other children do not think that the apparent respiratory ailment is communicable.

Epilepsy

Epileptic children are discussed in this chapter, since this condition is a cerebral dysfunction. Epilepsy is a condition requiring medication and management rather than physical habilitation.

Because of the nature of the seizures, epilepsy can be frightening. The best-known seizure is the *grand mal,* the convulsion in which the individual falls and becomes unconscious. In *petit mal,* the individual loses consciousness only momentarily. There is no convulsion of the body, but the eyes stare and the eyelids twitch. In *psychomotor epilepsy,* one usually has short periods of amnesia. One stares, drops things, mumbles, and does not remember his actions. *Jacksonian epilepsy* begins with the convulsion on one side of the body, usually starting at the foot and working up to the arm.

The advance of medicine has made it possible for most epileptic children to remain in the regular classroom. The convulsions can be controlled by medication in eighty percent of the cases of epilepsy.

Epilepsy, like other defects and diseases, exists in varying degrees. One individual may be affected only mildly with a great time-lapse between seizures, while another one may have very frequent, violent attacks; there are others who will range between these extremes. This may be the only problem of the individual or may be one of many. Most attacks can be controlled by medication, and the individual affected is more often normal than not.

Causes, Age at Onset, Predisposing Factors

It seems that no one is sure as to the exact cause of epilepsy, but there does seem to be general agreement that the seizures are caused by some chemical reaction within the brain that affects the nerves and muscles. A great deal of study has been done as to why some people are susceptible. Most authorities think that there has been an injury to some part of the brain that could have happened during the pre–, para–, or postnatal periods.

Prenatal causes could be hereditary, parental infections, anoxia, injury to the brain, diabetes, and excessive x ray. Paranatal factors could be anoxia, injury by forceps, prolonged labor, the Rh factor, and prematurity. Postnatal causes could arise from anoxia, trauma, infections, tumors, and injuries caused by accidents.

With some epileptics, there seem to be precipitating factors that cause seizures. Some of these factors are emotional shock, childhood fears, parental and peer rejection, and severe frustrations.

If the child's seizures are controlled, and he is not multiply handicapped, then he can function adequately in the regular classroom. Even if the child should have a seizure, the regular class teacher should know what to do in an emergency. First of all, the teacher should remain calm and not frighten the children. Next, s/he should turn the child's head to the side so that he will not choke on saliva, and s/he should make sure that the child does not swallow his tongue.

Rheumatic Fever

Rheumatic fever ranks as one of the major infectious diseases of childhood and early adolescence. Though it is not the dreaded disease that it has been in the past, it still creates many serious health problems. The associated problems of a rheumatic heart account for about 50,000 deaths per year in the United States. Its prevention and treatment continue to present a challenge to the medical profession.

Definition and Etiology

Rheumatic fever is a chronic inflammatory disease which is characterized by fever and swelling of the joints. The exact pathogenesis of the disease is not known, but it has been observed that it follows infection with the first group β-hemolytic Streptococcus. Studies on selected populations have shown that 3 percent of individuals with untreated first group streptococcal infection develop rheumatic fever (Hughes, 1967).

Many mild cases of rheumatic fever occur and are unrecognized. This mild condition in children is often called *growing pains*. However, the pains of these two conditions can be distinguished by noting that generally growing pains are in the muscles and occur at night. The pain of rheumatic fever is in the joints. The term *rheumatic fever* emphasizes the inflamed condition of the joints. This, however, is of secondary importance. The most serious implication of rheumatic fever is involvement of the heart. This condition could lead to permanent disability or death.

The original infection of first group Streptococcus is usually mild, and the resulting rheumatic fever may not cause heart damage. However, reinfection is common and often more severe. The frequent result of infection is damage to the heart.

The sequence in rheumatic fever ordinarily follows a pattern of three steps. There is an initial infection with first group β-hemolytic Streptococcus, such, as is present in scarlet fever, respiratory tract infections, and sore throat. This is followed by a latent period of one to three weeks. The third step is the onset of rheumatic fever.

Incidence

Rheumatic fever is a disease of childhood, occurring chiefly between the ages of five and fifteen. The disease is rare in the first four years of life and becomes rare again during the adult years. The high incidence of streptococcal infection during childhood and early adolescence seem directly related. When there is a high incidence of streptococcal infection in the adult population, an outbreak of rheumatic fever is a common result.

There are no reliable figures which give the incidence of rheumatic fever in the general population. The disease is not always recognized and reported to the physician. Commonly used as a reasonable index is the incidence of 3 percent of the untreated streptococcal cases. This has been decreasing for several years as has the incidence of streptococcal infection. The associated problems of rheumatic heart disease present the more serious problems.

As implied previously, all children who have rheumatic fever do not have rheumatic heart disease, and all children who have had heart murmurs are not necessarily ill. Rheumatic fever is serious, because it generally requires long periods of convalescence and is responsible for approximately 90 percent of the defective hearts in children. All teachers should be alerted to the symptoms of rheumatic fever.

After an attack, the period of treatment during convalescence may be long. During this time, the child will need a great deal of parental support and also home instruction from an itinerant teacher.

When the child returns to the regular classroom, there will be a few adjustments in curriculum and various types of activities permitted. However, the teacher's greatest responsibility is the prevention of reinfection and not a limitation of physical activity. The American Heart Association (1963) lists the following classifications that most physicians will refer to the school.

Functional Capacity

CLASS I. Patients with cardiac disease, but without resulting limitation of physical activity; ordinary physical activity does not cause undue fatigue, palpitation, dyspnea, or anginal pain.

CLASS II. Patients with cardiac disease resulting in slight limitation of physical activity; they are comfortable at rest. Ordinary physical activity results in fatigue, palpitation, dyspnea, or anginal pain.

CLASS III. Patients with cardiac disease resulting in marked limitation of physical activity; they are comfortable at rest. Less than ordinary activity causes fatigue, palpitation, dyspnea or anginal pain.

CLASS IV. Patients with cardiac disease resulting in inability to carry on any physical activity without discomfort; symptoms of cardiac insufficiency or of the anginal syndrome may be present even at rest. If any physical activity is undertaken, discomfort is increased.

Therapeutic Classification

CLASS A. Patients with cardiac disease whose physical activity need not be restricted.

CLASS B. Patients with cardiac disease whose ordinary physical activity need not be restricted, but who should be advised against severe or competitive physical efforts.

CLASS C. Patients with cardiac disease whose ordinary physical activity should be moderately restricted, and whose more strenuous efforts should be discontinued.

CLASS D. Patients with cardiac disease whose ordinary physical activity should be markedly restricted.

CLASS E. Patients with cardiac disease who should be at complete rest, confined to bed or chair.

Allergies

Eyes watery? Feel a sneeze coming on? Hand itching? If so, then you may be allergic to the paper you are holding. People are allergic to paper, the dust that may have accumulated on the edges of a book, or anything under the sun—including the sun itself.

If one can be allergic to anything, then just what is an allergy? Allergy is an acquired, specific, altered capability to react, based on an antigen-antibody reaction (Harris and Shure, 1969). Most people can eat bananas, strawberries, or other foods without worry. Most of us can breathe house dust without problems, but those who do have these problems are showing an "altered" or unusual reaction.

An *antigen* is a substance that enters the body and triggers the allergic reaction and symptoms. *Allergen* is often used as a synonym for *antigen.* Some common antigens are house dust, pollen, feathers, and mold, but as previously stated, they may be anything from the living room carpet to the kitchen sink cleanser. Antigens may enter the body through touch, inhalation, or ingestion. Either complete or incomplete, complete antigens are able to produce antibodies and to unite with them to cause the allergic reaction, incomplete antigens cannot perform both functions.

What are the most common allergy problems? If hay fever comes quickly to mind, that is correct; some other common allergies are bronchial asthma, eczema, urticaria or hives, and insect and drug allergies. A closer look at those common allergies—their causes and treatment—will be taken.

Hay Fever

During the seventeenth century, doctors thought the symptoms of sneezing, runny nose, and watery eyes were brought on by an emotional upset. For a long time afterward, the same symptoms occurring during rose-blooming time were called *rose fever.* Even later, these same symptoms occurring during the haying season in England came to be called *hay fever.* Although it is scientifically incorrect, the name has persisted. The correct term is *allergic rhinitis.*

Bronchial Asthma

Bottomly (1968) characterizes bronchial asthma as a clinically recognizable type of wheezing and difficulty in breathing caused by narrowing of the smallest branches of the bronchial tubes throughout both lungs and by the presence of tenacious mucus in these smallest branches. Often, in its early stages, it occurs as isolated and reversible attacks relieved by adrenalin or related drugs. Asthma attacks brought on by factors outside the body are said to have *extrinsic* causes: medicines, food, or pollen. *Intrinsic* causes are those which stem from inside the body: infections or a highly disturbed emotional state.

Skin Allergies

The skin is the largest and one of the most important organs of the body. It is also one of the most sensitive organs and is vulnerable to allergic reactions through touch or the blood-stream. The most common skin allergies are hives (urticaria) and eczema (atopic dermatitis).

Hives consist of white or reddish wheals and welts that itch, sting, and prick. Hives may attack a specific area of the body or spread over all areas. The trunk, buttocks, and chest are the parts of the body most frequently affected. Sometimes hives are com-bined with other diseases, such as eczema. Causes of hives include bacteria from infections in any part of the body; foods; drugs; inhalants in any season, time, or place; contactants of any sort; and the elements of heat, wind, light, or cold.

Reactions to Biting and Stinging Insects

It is normal to experience localized swelling, redness, and itching following the bite or sting of an insect. It is abnormal to experience flushing and swelling of the face and neck, fits of sneezing, watering of the eyes, coughing, and difficulty in breath-ing. These symptoms constitute an altered or allergic reaction to insect stings or bites.

Drug Allergies

Although it is expected that drugs will cause a reaction in the body of the user, an unusual and unexpected reaction to a par-ticular drug is an allergic reaction. Drugs are powerful foreign substances to which the body is not accustomed and should naturally be used with extreme care. The United States Food and Drug Administration has strict labeling laws regarding possible adverse reactions to nonprescription medications. Doctors and pharmacists are well informed concerning prescription drugs.

Most children suffering from allergies do not need special edu-cational planning unless they are hospitalized or homebound. The regular classroom teacher must be constantly alerted to the fact that if a child has an allergic attack, the home should be notified immediately. If the child does not have other disabilities hindering educational achievement, he will be able to participate like normal children.

Tuberculosis

Tuberculosis is one of the oldest diseases known to man. Evidence of tuberculosis has been found in Egyptian mummies dating as far back as 1000 B.C. The "white plague" has killed millions of humans within recorded history. Wars, famines, and pestilences have not equalled its terrible toll of death and sickness. For centuries, it has been one of the world's biggest killers.

Today, medical science has the means to eradicate tuberculosis. It can be eliminated as a major public health problem in the United States through the application of modern-day techniques. It is recognized that this multifaceted program will take many years and have to have intermediate goals along the way.

In the United States, there are an estimated 25 million people infected by tubercle bacilli. While they are not sick, they have living TB germs in their bodies and may develop the active disease. Over 1.5 million of these have actually been ill with the disease. An estimated 2 million will develop it in their lifetime unless it is prevented. Today approximately 250,000 Americans have active tuberculosis; another 550,000 have the disease in an inactive form and should be under medical supervision. In 1969, for example, there were 4,729 known cases of tuberculosis in the small state of Arkansas, 563 of which were newly reported cases.

Tuberculosis is more prevalent in urban slums, because it spreads easily in a crowded, poorly ventilated environment. The infection rate for school entrants run as high as 3 percent in some slum areas, whereas in 1969, the national average was 0.3 percent. But the well housed, and well fed get TB, too; suburbanites and rural dwellers. People of any age are susceptible.

Unlike other infectious and communicable diseases, tuberculosis infection is not an active sickness, but it can become so. A person may be infected as long as forty or more years before the disease becomes active. More new cases in the next few years will be people who are not infected. Also, immunity is not acquired by having tuberculosis. Even though recovered, the tuberculosis victim may have a relapse.

Tuberculosis is primarily an airborne infectious disease caused by the tubercle bacillus *Mycobacterium tuberculosis.* Persons become infected by breathing germs from an infectious patient. TB germs get into the air in contaminated droplets coughed, sneezed, talked, or laughed by a person with active tuberculosis. One cough may broadcast thousands of germs. They can be spread by contaminated articles, too. The natural defenses of the upper respiratory tract will filter out many of these germs, but some will get by and into the lungs. However, it usually takes prolonged exposure to an active case to become infected.

The lungs are a favorite spot of attack by TB germs, but they may strike any part of the body. The body counters with white cells that attempt to surround and destroy the germs. While the white cells are killing some germs, the body tries to enclose the invaders with a wall of cells and fibers. This reaction of the body creates a tiny lump, a *tubercle,* that gives the disease its name. These form six to eight weeks after the initial entry and slow down the bacilli. At first the tubercle is soft and looks fuzzy, but it gradually hardens into a scar. Millions of people go through life with tubercles containing live germs in their lungs without ever getting sick.

Children with tuberculosis of the bones or joints require a program consisting of relatively physical inactivity for a long period of time. The number of children so afflicted has been reduced because of new drugs and surgical procedures. Children having tuberculosis have the need to attend hospital schools and later need home instruction. After the condition has been arrested, the child returns to the regular classroom.

Diabetes

For hundreds of years, man had recorded facts and feelings concerning the disease known as *diabetes.* Why should the average man know about diabetes? The answer is simple: One of the most common diseases today, diabetes affects about 4 million persons in the United States, and estimates indicate that another $5\frac{1}{2}$ million are potential diabetics. More than $1\frac{1}{2}$ million of the 4 million are unaware that they have the disease. The possibility of becoming a diabetic increases with age and other known circumstances. Furthermore, medical progress has made it possible to more adequately control the ailment, or possibly avoid it, when it is diagnosed in its early stages.

What is Diabetes?

Diabetes mellitus is a disease affecting the metabolic functions of the body. The carbohydrate intake of the body fails to "burn" properly, and an excess of glucose accumulates in the blood-stream. This condition is known as *hyperglycemia*. The excess glucose is drained away in the urine, and this condition is *glycosuria*.

Carbohydrates are the starch and sugar foods on which the body depends for its main source of energy. Foods are used immediately to supply heat and energy, or they may be stored in the body for future use. In normal functioning, the body makes use of these carbohydrates, but in diabetes this is not the case. The inability of the body to utilize certain foods causes the excess glucose to accumulate in the blood and the kidneys work overtime to excrete the sugar via urine. In this light, diabetes may be considered more a condition than a disease, since it is not something one "catches."

Discovery of Insulin

Scientist Paul Langerhans discovered a cluster of cells in the pancreas unlike the other tissues of the organ. Although this section of the pancreas, the islets of Langerhans, bears his name, the significance of these cells was not known for some time after the discovery. It is the pancreas which secretes the necessary elements for utilization of the carbohydrates in the body. In 1921, F. G. Banting, a Canadian doctor, and C. H. Best, a graduate medical student, discovered insulin. It is this hormone, produced in the islets of Langerhans, that makes it possible for the body to convert the starches and sugars into the heat and energy it needs. Inadequate or faulty conversion of these substances can result in an imbalance between the food eaten and the metabolic needs of the body. The diabetic has the foods present, but cannot use them. Since the body must have energy to live it turns on itself, developing poisons in the system that give rise to coma and, eventually, death. Untreated with insulin or one of the newer oral drugs, diabetes is fatal.

Symptoms

Since the kidneys are working overtime to remove the excess sugar from the blood of the diabetic, s/he is likely to urinate frequently. This constant fluid loss from the body causes excessive thirst. It is likely that the diabetic will also be weak, listless, and hungry. The food s/he eats is not properly assimilated by the body; hence, the diabetic may begin to lose weight, no matter how much food he consumes. Other symptoms related to the imbalance in his system may be changes in vision, slow healing process, itching, pain in the fingers and toes, and/or drowsiness.

In less severe cases, only a few of these symptoms may occur. In fact, the diabetic is usually overweight for a time before a noticeable weight loss begins. In many cases, diabetes is discovered before any of these symptoms appear, if the person undergoes a regular medical checkup.

Educational Implications

Special schools are not required for the diabetic child, but patient and understanding teachers are definitely an asset. The nature of diabetes in childhood may require midmorning snacks to prevent insulin reactions. The erratic spilling of sugar into the urine may necessitate frequent trips from the classroom. Such manifestations may prove painfully embarrassing to the already sensitive child and cause humiliation before a class. An understanding teacher can handle such situations with a minimum of embarrassment to the child.

As the diabetic child progresses to the upper grades, this symptom-sensitivity lessens, and the problem becomes more one of scheduling. Physical education classes must be arranged so that they will not place excessive strain on a diabetic child's insulino-genic functions. Teachers are often poorly informed or shamefully ignorant of the symptoms and control of diabetes and its accompanying problems. Although some teachers make an effort to learn about the needs of their diabetic students, it is frequently beneficial to have a doctor's statement of the child's specific medical needs and his ability to participate in sports or other forms of exercise.

The greatest problem for the teacher of an insulin-dependent diabetic is recognizing and counteracting insulin reaction. A teacher can provide additional support to the child's normal group adjustment by being aware, informed, and prepared for emergencies.

REFERENCES

Bottomly, H.W.: *Allergy: Its Treatment and Care.* New York, Funk & W, 1968.

Harris, M.C. and Shure, N.: *All About Allergy.* Englewood Cliffs, P-H, 1969.

Hughes, J.G.: *Synopsis of Pediatrics,* 2nd ed. St. Louis, Mosby, 1967.

Chapter 3

EDUCATIONAL AND PSYCHOLOGICAL TESTING OF THE PHYSICALLY HANDICAPPED

T HE REHABILITATION of the physically impaired individual has become an increasing concern for psychologists and educators during the past decade. The score and quality of the services received by the handicapped is as important as the number of individuals receiving these services.

EDUCATIONAL AND PSYCHOLOGICAL EVALUATIONS

Actual disabilities handicap an individual, but the person's self-concept can be as crippling as the actual physical handicap. Because of the sensitivity to physical handicaps, psychological and educational testing must be administered in a manner that produces valid results.

There is a direct relationship between physical deficit and personal adjustment. Physical handicaps are often medical problems with psychological and educational aspects. The obstacles that the disability interposes may be psychological, as well as educational.

Selection of Tests

All testing with the handicapped must take into consideration the individual's ability to see, speak, hear, write, or otherwise respond to directions. The severity of the disablement influences the test results, if the speech is impaired. As in any valid and reliable test, the examiner must be well versed in the performance of the nonhandicapped on identical tests.

The selection of suitable tests is determined by the examiner in instances where speech and motor dexterity are present. The subject's verbal comprehension may influence the selecting of a test. Modifications in administering standard tests become necessary when the more than moderately physically involved individual is present.

Educational Testing

Educational testing of physically handicapped children varies from regular teacher-made tests and standardized tests, to specifically individualized teacher-made tests. For example, the severely involved cerebral palsied child, who can only nod his head, can give responses to a teacher who has a communication system set up between his– or herself and the youngster. Some children are able to communicate by moving a lever that lights a board, and others are able to communicate only by typing on a typewriter with their toes.

The teacher must evaluate each child individually and use all of her experience to determine the level of the child's functioning. It must be pointed out also that, regardless of what a child knows, he must be able to function with nonhandicapped individuals if he is to be productive. True ability becomes less important if the individual involved cannot function in the American society with other nonhandicapped individuals. Teachers should always explain to the parents what she thinks the child's true ability is in reading, arithmetic, and social studies, etc., but she should also tell the parents how the child functions when compared with nonhandicapped children.

Psychological Testing

When discussing the psychological evaluation of children with handicaps, it must be noted at once that this group is large, and it is a group with commonly divergent characteristics. The causes of handicaps are many, and the results vary according to the cause.

The concern of primary importance in dealing with evaluating these children is that applied tests and measurements are set up for and standardized on a group of normal children. Because handicapped children undeniably have physical problems, in many cases (particularly with such problems as cerebral palsy), at least a chance of neurological impairment exists.

Problems In Testing

The greatest problem when applying tests to handicapped children and then interpreting the results obtained is that one cannot be sure whether a low score on an intelligence test is a result of low intelligence or poor responding ability because of the child's handicap.

If the child is being treated with anticonvulsant drugs, this may be a distorting factor in his test performance. It is important also to remember that perceptual and spatial disabilities occur very frequently in certain kinds of cerebral palsy and that these are not necessarily in keeping with overall intellectual level (Wolf and Anderson, 1965).

Cruickshank (1971) speculates that the handicapped child may be involved with a success-prohibitory situation: "The handicap sets into operation a circular situation: The handicap is the barrier to success; frustration results; attempts are made to substitute satisfactions for the original activity; the handicap is again a barrier; greater frustration results; more activity; more blocking ad infinitum."

Emotional Adjustment of Handicapped Children

Kanner (1972) postulates that this does not suggest that emotional disturbance is a characteristic of physically handicapped children. Allen and Pearson (1938) found that the personalities of some children with physical defects are not affected by their trouble; those who reacted with feelings of shame, inferiority, inability to face difficult situations, a desire to be in the center of attention, and actual or fancied overcompensation had causes other than the physical defect alone.

In an old project concerning emotional adjustment of physically handicapped children, Kammerer (1940) studied fifty patients with scoliosis and thirty with osteomyelitis. An analysis of the results of the Rogers Test of Personality, to which they were submitted, failed to give any indication that the group of handicapped children was different from a normal one of similar age and composition. This study concluded that physical handicapping conditions may play a part in personality maladjustment, but presence of the defect alone does not appear to be sufficient to cause development of undesirable traits.

It has been suggested from some that the type and severity of handicap and the duration of the crippling element may be of considerable importance. In a somewhat dated, but still applicable study, Donofrio (1951) investigated the effects of crippling on intelligence, school achievement, and emotional adjustment for 270 physically handicapped children aged five through sixteen, who attended a special school. There were thirty-two different medical diagnoses for the sample; poliomyelitis was the most common. Among the findings were as follows:

1. Measured intellectual ability was within the normal range.
2. On the average, these children were achieving up to their estimated mental potential.
3. Emotional adjustment appeared to fall within the normal range.

Adjustment, evaluated by the Brown Personality Inventory and by teacher rating, was found to improve with age and was better among the less severely involved children.

In a study which took place about twenty years ago, Kimmel studied thirty children of both sexes, between ten and sixteen years old, who were treated on an outpatient basis at a New York hospital. In the test were fifteen individuals who were listed as the congenital and fifteen placed in the acquired group.

All subjects were given the Rorschach and the Figure Drawing tests. The test results showed that the acquired group showed significantly greater body confidence and esteem. The congenital group used projection as a defense mechanism significantly more than the acquired group.

No significant differences were found in reported instances of adjustment difficulties in areas of family, school, and social relations. Duration and severity of disability were not found related to lack of body confidence or anxiety in either group (Cruickshank, 1971).

Physical Limitations

The nature of certain tests make them patently unsuitable for psychological evaluation of physically handicapped children. Tests that rely heavily on physical reactions or responses work a hardship on handicapped children who may not be able to produce the required physical responses.

Cruickshank, in 1966, wrote that the method used in examining a child varies according to his physical condition. There is, in many cases, no need whatsoever to modify test administration in the least. A large percentage of children with cerebral palsy are able to talk well enough to be understood easily. Thus, administering verbal tests is a comparatively simple matter, assuming the pertinent sensory modalities are intact. Many cerebral-palsied children also have at least one good hand, and so are able to manage the blocks, cards, and other material of which performance tests are composed.

In the same book, Cruickshank states when physical limitations are more serious, it often becomes necessary to make adaptations or adjustments to the test and the testing situation. At the outset, the examiner must choose the type of test which can be administered with the least modification. If the subject has good hands and poor speech, performance tests are appropriate. If the opposite is true, verbal tests may have priority. In the majority of cases, the examiner will be able to give at least part of both of these types of tests.

On occasion, a child can tell the examiner what to do, although he cannot do it himself. This could occur on the maze items in the Binet scale, or on the mazes of the Wechsler Intelligence Scale for Children-Revised (WISC-R).

Caution is advised in modification of psychological tests, no matter what the nature of the modification may be. "If intelligence test scores are to continue to mean anything, the test must be given and scored strictly in accordance with the rubric. Should the examiner feel that he would get some additional and helpful data by doing something other than strict administration this should be done apart from the normal test situation . . . and such "results" should be recorded in a separate comment" (Wolf and Anderson, 1965) .

An acceptable modification of the testing procedure that may be used on certain tests is the use of pantomime. A response given in pantomime may be accepted if the effort is so good that there can be no doubt about the adequacy of the answer. Many of the Binet absurdities can be answered in this way. The Hiskey-Nebraska Test makes good use of pantomime in giving directions (Hiskey, 1966) .

Some tests can be used as though they were multiple choice in nature. Arithmetic problems, for example, frequently can be administered in this way.

Testing procedure is not the only facet of psychological evaluation of handicapped children that can be modified. The test materials can be modified to fit specific situations. A child who cannot pick up small blocks or pieces of puzzles may be able to handle large ones. Even a piece of wood as small as a matchstick can be glued to a piece of movable material, which may make it possible for a child to solve a form board problem. The examiner must, however, be aware that by attaching the matchstick he has modified and perhaps increased the complexity and difficulty of the test. Also, s/he may have made the task too easy.

As a final note involving modification of test procedures and materials, again emphasis should be placed on restraint. Changing the test changes the form and results of whatever test is being administered. Before a test is changed, care should be taken to insure that the changes are absolutely necessary to get an accurate score and the test is changed to the minimum required.

The first part of this chapter dealt primarily with general descriptions of characteristics of physically handicapped children found in some studies involving psychological evaluation. Also, the adjustments most commonly made on standardized psychological tests were examined in some detail. The second part of this chapter deals with those tests most commonly administered in the evaluation of orthopedically handicapped children.

EVALUATION OF ORTHOPEDICALLY
HANDICAPPED CHILDREN

In research the tests commonly used and usually best for evaluating orthopedically handicapped children are those that rely primarily upon verbal responses. However, a universally accepted list of psychological tests for handicapped children unfortunately does not exist. It appears that there are objections about nearly every test now available, as well as points which are favored. Some authorities provide some tests they suggest are better suited for handicapped children than other tests.

Denhoff's List of Tests

Denhoff (1960) supplies some tests that he feels provide more valid information and are most used in current clinical studies of cerebral palsied and other physically handicapped children. This list includes The Revised Stanford-Binet, form L or M; the Wechsler Intelligence Scale for Children; the Vineland Social Maturity Scale; the Goodenough Draw-A-Man; the Columbia Mental Maturity Scale; and Raven's Progressive Matrices (Denhoff and Robinault, 1960). It is assumed that since the Wechsler test has been restandardized after the publication date of this book by Denhoff, Denhoff would most probably include the revision on his list of most acceptable and usable tests.

Stanford-Binet Test

Jessie Francis-Williams evaluates the Stanford-Binet test as best for assessing physically handicapped children.

Despite the fact that many cerebral palsied children (and other crippled children) suffer motor handicaps and the deprivation caused by sensory defects and limited opportunities for normal "learning" as well as for social experiences, the Stanford-Binet Intelligence test for assessing the intelligence level of those cerebral palsied children whose speech can be understood or who can make clear, even though in a most limited way, what their response to questions and tasks is (Wolf and Anderson, 1965).

WISC-R

The Wechsler Intelligence Scale for Children—Revised is of more limited usefulness as an overall test of general intelligence for cerebral palsied children, since the Performance Scale has so many timed tests in which a child with a motor handicap and poor motor coordination inevitably scores badly. The Block Designs and Object Assembly subtests present serious difficulties to children with spatial and perceptual problems.

Peabody Picture Vocabulary Test

The Peabody Picture Vocabulary Test has been noted by many authorities as a very good test to be used on physically handicapped children. Cruickshank (1966) evaluates the Peabody as being very beneficial. He says as follows:

> This test has certain obvious advantages for use with exceptional children. It does not require that the subject read, point, or necessarily make oral responses. It is only essential that the subject indicate yes or no in some manner that the examiner can understand. The pictures do not include fine detail, thus minimizing figure-ground reversal problems. These physical features of the test, of course, commend its use with nonreaders, or poor readers, or speech handicapped and motor-involved youngsters.

It would seem that the Peabody test might be best utilized in situations where the child has rather gross problems in motor response or in speech formation.

Reliability and Validity of Tests

A question which must of necessity be asked about psychological evaluation of physically handicapped children, no matter what instrument is being used, is whether the test is a good, reliable measure of the child's abilities and whether or not the test is a valid predictor of the child's future progress. All psychological tests attempt to do these things, and the tests which are given to children who have physical handicaps are no different. The only difference is one of judging if the child has been able to respond to a test with his best effort.

In an effort to try to determine the statistical agreement between the test results of certain handicapped children and their actual progress, a group of researchers conducted a survey. In a study of fifty young cerebral-palsied children, Denhoff, Helden, and Silver found that there was an 81 percent agreement between psychological test prediction and actual clinical progress over a two-year period, which was statistically far beyond chance. These researchers used the revised Stanford-Binet test (form L) on all children who could respond at a one-and-one-half-year-old level and the Vineland Social Maturity Scale on those infants or children unable to respond to the Stanford-Binet test (Denhoff and Robinault, 1960).

As a result of this study, and other studies, it is Denhoff's opinion that ". . . in probably 90 percent of all cases (of physically handicapping conditions among children) at least an estimate of the general level of ability can be ascertained through careful attention to the subject's responses, limited though they may be" (Denhoff and Robinault, 1960).

Importance of Studies on Tests

The primary importance of the Denhoff study (1960) was that it lends strength to the argument of those who felt psychological testing of handicapped children was a sound practice, especially for educational purposes. This study tended to show that there was a definite relationship between the test results of these children and their actual progress.

Further substantiation of the contention that the present psychological scales are adequate for evaluating physically handicapped children are seen in the other studies.

Dunn and Harley, in a comparison of the results yielded by the Peabody Picture Vocabulary, the Ammons, the Van Alstyne, and the Columbia Mental Maturity tests found results similar in many ways to the Denhoff study. They concluded that all four tests had utility as predictors of the school success of children with cerebral palsy.

The Peabody and the Ammons seemed to be the tests which were useful with a wider range of age-groups than the other two tests examined. In fact, the Van Alstyne seemed applicable to children whose mental ages were above four years.

In another study, Ando (1968), when comparing the values for the cerebral palsied of the Peabody Picture Vocabulary Test with the Verbal Scale of the Wechsler Intelligence Scale for Children, found the two instruments to be highly correlated (Cruickshank, 1971).

A very beneficial point can be seen from the Ando study. The Wechsler test is probably the most commonly used and best-known test in the public schools for psychological evaluation. Since the Verbal Scale compares well with the Peabody test in Ando's study, it would seem that it is a good argument for administering this part of the Wechsler to handicapped children. For schools with a low budget for psychological testing, this could represent some savings of funds.

From the studies examined above, it would appear that testing for physically handicapped children is a valid and profitable undertaking and that good usable results can be found from using present tests.

Extreme views have been expressed, such as that cerebral-palsied children are not testable at all. On the other hand, certain real limitations in psychological assessment sometimes have been so minimized as to suggest that there need be no modifications in test procedures at all. Each of these views may be true in some cases, but neither is correct in the majority.

The intellectual functioning level of probably 90 percent of all physically handicapped children can be diagnosed with a good degree of validity, and particularly within such wide categories as superior, average, mentally retarded, and mentally deficient. Short-term predictions as to a child's intellectual progress during the subsequent two- or three-year period can usually be made. Longer-term predictions are subject to the same limitations and liability to error as any other case (Denhoff and Robinault, 1960).

Multidiscipline Approach to Assessment

The number and kind of assessment techniques available for psychoeducational diagnosis of the physically handicapped are many and varied. Many techniques are shared among various disciplines, particularly psychology, education, pediatrics, and the language specialties.

The search for an assessment packet specific to children with physical handicaps is unproductive, because the diversity of learning and behavior symptoms may be manifested differently in different children and at different ages. Therefore, the selection of useful and appropriate tools should be determined through a reasoning process that takes into account the degree and kind of physical impairment, the age of the child, data from other sources, objectives of the diagnosis, availability of social services, and placement possibilities.

The following is a list of many tests which could be used in the psychoeducational diagnosis of the physically handicapped. These tests have been suggested by Clements and Hicks (1974).

Developmental Screening Methods

BAYLEY SCALES OF INFANT DEVELOPMENT. These are mental and motor scales for the assessment of early mental and psychomotor development of infants and young children (for ages 2 months to 2.6 years).

DENVER DEVELOPMENTAL SCREENING TEST. This test assesses development in the four areas of gross motor, fine motor, language, and personal-social responsiveness (for ages 2 weeks to 6.4 years).

DEVELOPMENTAL SCREENING INVENTORY FOR INFANTS. The development in the five areas of gross and fine motor, adaptive, language, and personal-social is measured by this test (for ages four weeks to eighteen months).

GESELL DEVELOPMENTAL SCHEDULES. The development in the four areas of motor, adaptive, language, and personal-social are tested (for ages four weeks to four years).

CATTELL INFANT INTELLIGENCE SCALE. This is a modified downward extension of the Stanford-Binet Intelligence Scale (for ages three to thirty months).

Measures of Global Intelligence

STANFORD-BINET INTELLIGENCE SCALE. (Combined L and M Form). The Standford-Binet is an individually administered test of intelligence for ages two through eighteen years.

WECHSLER PRESCHOOL AND PRIMARY SCALE OF INTELLIGENCE (WPPSI). An individually administered test of intelligence for ages 4.0 to 6.6 years, the Wechsler provides separate scales for verbal and performance tasks.

WECHSLER INTELLIGENCE SCALE FOR CHILDREN — REVISED (WISC-R). This is an individually administered test of intelligence for ages 5.0 to 15.11 years, which provides separate scales for verbal and performance tasks.

HISKEY-NEBRASKA TEST OF LEARNING APTITUDE. This is a mental ability assessment that can be given to hearing and non-hearing children. Parts of this test are particularly good for the physically handicapped, because it utilizes pantomime in giving directions, and most of the test is untimed. This is especially good if the child has average hand-eye coordination.

Global Academic-related Measures

LANGUAGE AND LEARNING DISORDERS OF THE PREACADEMIC CHILD: WITH CURRICULUM GUIDE (Bangs, 1966). This includes assessment tools for language skills, avenues of learning, and pre-academic curriculum guides for age six months through kindergarten.

THE PRESCHOOL INVENTORY. This is a series of tasks which measure achievement in the four areas of personal-social responsiveness, associative vocabulary, numerical concept activation, and sensory concept activation (for use with ages three years to six years).

THE MEETING STREET SCHOOL SCREENING TEST. An individually administered series of tests for the early identification of children with learning disabilities, this includes a behavior rating scale (for use with children ages 5.0 to 7.5 years).

PREDICTING READING FAILURE (de Hirsch et al., 1966). This book includes a series of ten tests which constitute The Predictive Index for identifying kindergarten age children with high potential for reading disability.

SCHOOL READINESS (Ilg and Ames, 1964) contains a series of techniques for assessing developmental levels of children within the age-range of five to ten years.

Measures of Visual-Motor Skills

FROSTIG DEVELOPMENTAL TESTS OF VISUAL PERCEPTION. A perceptual quotient determined from the child's performance on subtests which include eye/hand coordination, figure-ground discrimination, form constancy, position in space, and spatial relationships, is provided (for use with children aged three to ten years).

BERRY-BUKTENICA VISUAL-MOTOR INTEGRATION TEST. This gives an estimation of visual perceptual functioning through the copying of geometric forms (for use within the age-range of two to fifteen years).

BENDER VISUAL-MOTOR GESTALT TEST. This test measures the maturational level of visual-motor development in preschool and school-age children.

LINCOLN-OSERETSKY MOTOR DEVELOPMENT SCALE. Thirty-six tasks measure general motor proficiency of children (for use with ages six to fourteen years).

AYRES SPACE TEST. This is a performance test which measures visual-perceptual speed, spatial ability, and position in space (for use with ages three to ten years).

PURDUE PERCEPTUAL-MOTOR SURVEY (Roach and Kephart, 1966). This volume has a variety of assessment techniques for indicating the level of perceptual-motor development in children.

Measures of Language Skills

ILLINOIS TEST OF PSYCHOLINGUISTIC ABILITIES (ITPA). Abilities, along the three dimensions of communication channels (audiovocal and visuomotor), psycholinguistic processes (receptive, organization, and expressive), and levels of organization (automatic and representational) are evaluated (for use with ages two to ten years).

WEPMAN AUDITORY DISCRIMINATION TEST. The Wepman assesses the auditory discrimination ability of children within the age-range of five to eight years.

REFERENCES

Bangs, T.: *Language and Learning Disorders of the Pre-academic Child: With Curriculum Guide.* New York, Appleton, 1968.

Clements, S.D. and Hicks, T.J.: Physically and neurologically impaired. In Wisland, M.V. (Ed.): *Psychoeducational Diagnosis of Exceptional Children.* Springfield, Thomas, 1974.

Cruickshank, W.M.: *Cerebral Palsy — Its Individual and Community Problems.* Syracuse, Syracuse U Pr, 1966.

Cruickshank, W.M.: *Psychology of Exceptional Children and Youth.* Englewood Cliffs, P-H, 1971.

de Hirsch, K. et al.: *Predicting Reading Failure.* New York, Har-Row, 1966.

Denhoff, E. and Robinault, I.P.: *Cerebral Palsy and Related Disorders,* New York, McGraw, 1960.

Ilg, F.L. and Ames, L.B.: *School Readiness: Behavioral Tests Used at the Gesell Institute.* New York, Har-Row, 1964.

Kanner, L.: *Child Psychiatry.* Springfield, Thomas, 1972.

Roach, E. and Kephart, N.: *Purdue Perceptual-Motor Survey.* Columbus, Merrill, 1966.

Wolf, J. and Anderson, R.M.: *The Multiply Handicapped Child.* Springfield, Thomas, 1965.

Chapter 4

TEACHING LANGUAGE ARTS AND MATH TO ORTHOPEDICALLY HANDICAPPED CHILDREN

THE PAST generation has seen a rapid development in educational services adapted to meet the needs of orthopedically handicapped children. The right of each child to be provided with the instruction and training he requires to make the most of his/her possibilities is recognized, whether those possibilities be great or small. It is recognized, too, that adequate teaching methods should be adapted to prepare for a more successful future those children who deviate from the normal so seriously that they cannot participate in regular classroom activities.

The purpose of this chapter is to discuss the language arts and math curriculum of the orthopedically handicapped child.

Adaptive Teaching Methods

In teaching the multiply handicapped child, certain adaptive teaching methods must be employed in order to build an effective program.

The handicapped child presents a picture of incomplete and uneven development. For example, a child with severe motor disability may have the physical strength and competence of an infant, and yet, this same child may be able to use language for communicating and for gaining knowledge of his environment. Another child may have good motor skills and be fairly independent in all the activities of daily living, but because of severe speech impairment, he may communicate largely through gestures and auditory clues to orient himself with his environment (Schattner, 1971).

Paraplegia

In this chapter, when the paraplegic child is discussed, the author is referring to a child who has only lower-body involvement and full control over his upper extremities. There are many causes of *paraplegia*. Some of these would include spina bifida, cerebral palsy, poliomyelitis, spinal meningitis, and paralysis due to accidents.

The author refers to a *hemiplegic* as a child or person with some motor loss on one side of his body. Hemiplegia may be caused by strokes, tumors, accidents, toxins, and viruses, etc. There will be certain adaptive techniques discussed to help compensate for the motor loss. Because of the involvement of all four limbs and often the absence of speech, *quadriplegics* will be discussed concerning why they most often require special adaptations of instruction. A common example of a quadriplegic would be a *cerebral-palsied child* with four limbs affected. Children with muscular and bone disorders require some special adaptive techniques primarily due to the lack of strength in their upper extremites. Muscular dystrophy and atrophy, arthritis, and osteogenesis imperfecta are some examples of these muscular and bone disorders. Children with artificial limbs present special problems, but often they can be dealt with in the manner as children that have other types of upper-extremity involvements.

Methods and Techniques to Compensate

This chapter deals with methods and techniques to help compensate for the motor losses suffered by the orthopedically handicapped child. The special techniques are needed more for children with upper-extremity involvement, since most conventional methods rely so heavily on the ability to manipulate and use the hands and arms.

In teaching language arts and math, loss of the use of the lower extremities presents no special handicap to the child's learning ability. However, special placement of these children is often required, not because of their intellectual differences, but to accommodate their toilet needs and physical plant requirements. However, for the child who does need special techniques, certain measures can be utilized to make his learning an enriching and successful experience.

TEACHING LANGUAGE ARTS

The language arts program is terribly inadequate for a large percentage of children having multiple handicaps. These children may be isolated in the hospital for long periods of time, brain damaged, or suffering from a severe speech impairment. All of these are contributing factors that lead to a failure of the language arts program. The language arts program for the handicapped child must, therefore, be an enriching experience.

This chapter must discuss five different phases of the language arts program and suggest creative and adaptive teaching techniques to be used with the different types of orthopedic handicaps. The areas of discussion are reading, English, writing, spelling, and social studies. Each area lists different types of instruction and describes the most effective for the orthopedically handicapped student.

Reading

From the experience of most teachers working with physically handicapped children, we have found no single, best method of teaching reading; even in a class with only eleven students, the physical and mental abilities are so diverse, several methods must be utilized to achieve the best results. Three methods of teaching reading which will be discussed are the basal approach, the multisensory approach, and the method of individualized instruction. The following suggestions are some passed on to the author by teachers who work with orthopedically handicapped children.

Basal Approach

It is the author's opinion the basal approach is a very effective method to use with some students. The year should be begun by using reading groups with as many of the students as possible. Reading groups are usually formed on the basis of school records and after teacher observations and assessments after several days of association with the new students. This approach should be used with children having near-average or above-average intelligence, so that the interest level of the reader will correspond with the age-level of the child. When teaching this method, it is best to have at least two or three children in a group. Group discussions and interpretations are very meaningful experiences for the students, and this type of approach builds both a structural and sequential program. By using supplementary materials, a sound program can be built to teach word attack skills, comprehension, phonics, oral reading, vocabulary, and the other skills of reading.

The handicapped students who benefit most from reading groups using the basal approach are paraplegics and children with muscular and bone disorders. These handicapped students do not require as many adaptive methods of teaching as do the remainder of the students. Often, they do not have any orthopedic disabilities that necessitate any unusual adaptations to the mode of reading instruction. However, one exception to consider is the extreme weakness that accompanies children with muscular disorders, such as muscular dystrophy and atrophy. These children generally need help in picking up their textbooks, opening their desks, and other skills which require muscular strength, but this problem is easily remediated. The muscular dystrophic child requires more and more help as he gets older. He may need special tables to give arm support, and as s/he becomes weaker, study notes must be made for him, or he must use a cassette tape recorder.

It is the teacher's responsibility to create a physical environment in the classroom allowing each handicapped child to function to the height of his physical capabilities. Therefore, a teacher should try to evaluate each child's handicap and arrange for him or her to have a desk and facilities that are easily operated. Osteogenesis imperfecta would also be another exception considering the strength of the student. This child might also need some assistance with heavy readers or textbooks to prevent the breaking of brittle bones, which is associated with this particular handicap.

With adaptations, children with upper-extremity involvement can be taught with the basal reader approach. Book holders are helpful to keep the book in place so the child can see the pages. Another method of keeping the page is to place a paper clip or clothes pin on it. Sometimes the child can learn to place his hand on the book to hold the correct page himself.

Many children, especially quadraplegics, who cannot write but can use a typewriter, can turn the workbook pages that accompany the series. When a child must use a typewriter, the teacher should have two workbooks available. Often when the workbook page is placed in the typewriter, the child cannot see all the printed material needed to complete the page. By having two workbooks available, one can be torn apart to be placed in the machine and the other can be placed where the child can read it.

Multisensory Approach

The author feels that the multisensory approach to reading would be extremely effective with paraplegics suffering from spina bifida and hemiplegics suffering from paralysis due to a stroke. Because of these specific orthopedic handicaps, these children are more likely to be brain damaged and have severe learning disabilities. These children, because of their physical handicaps, are not to be grouped with the learning-disabled child, as defined by educational guidelines. However, because of their brain damage, in addition to their physical handicap, these children will profit from the instruction outlined for the learning disabled child.

The typical brain-damaged child suffers from disturbances such as distractibility, perceptual disturbances, and thinking and behavior disorders. The author also feels that methods can be developed to relieve the perceptual and conceptual disturbances of brain-injured children. Visual, auditory, and kinesthetic approaches must be used in teaching reading to this child. According to some authorities, children learn 85 percent by visual stimuli, 11 percent by auditory stimuli, 2 percent by kinesthetic means, 3 percent by olfactory stimuli, and 1 percent by tasting.

Hammill and Myers (1969) find that brain damage, learning disabilities, hyperactivity, and poor fine-motor development are often associated with orthopedically handicapped children. One effective means of teaching reading to the brain-damaged and perceptually handicapped child would be to begin with oral phonetic instruction. The whole-word method is usually inadequate and must be reinforced by a strong phonics program. Symbols are used only after the child can discriminate sounds and reproduce them in isolation. After the child has developed fairly adequate auditory discrimination, the letter should be presented as the visual symbol for the sound.

Lehtinen finds it beneficial to assign a color to each vowel sound and to teach an association between color and sound. The words are written on paper, letter by letter, using a stamping set, or they are built by using letter cards. This method is sometimes effective for some orthopedically handicapped children, due to their poor fine-motor development. With some gross-motor ability, a child can build a word by himself and experience immediate success. Other suggestions that work well with the brain-damaged and perceptually handicapped child are letter puzzles and slotted word covers that expose only one word or sentence at a time. Pages in textbooks and workbooks loaded with distractions are not suitable for brain-damaged or perceptually handicapped children. However, they are valuable as supplementary work, if the pages are cut up and rearranged in a simpler fashion. If supplementary worksheets are used, they should be kept short for the extremely hyperactive child. Length and time involved to complete an assignment can gradually be increased according to the severity of hyperactivity.

It is also beneficial to eliminate other distractions for the brain-damaged, perceptually handicapped, and hyperactive child. The teacher should maintain a minimal amount of noise in the classroom. Noisy activities from other students in the classroom are very distracting to a hyperactive child. The visual and physical appearance of the classroom should not be cluttered or over decorated. These are only a few of the many techniques that can be applied to this special child. Once again, while teaching this method, many of the same adaptations discussed in the basal approach will have to be correlated in this program.

Individualized Program Approach

The medical diagnosis plays an important part in determining the individualized program for most students. Many conditions, as stated previously, have no associated learning problems and will need only regular curriculum at a slower rate, especially if they are frequently absent.

The individualized method of instruction is most productive in working with the severely involved child. Rita Weny of North Little Rock, Arkansas, has been associated with the teaching of orthopedically handicapped children for many years. She has been extremely effective in this area and has shared some of her special teaching ideas with the author. The following ideas on individualized instruction were developed by her.

If a teacher gets a student that is an extremely involved athetoid, she must first set up a way to communicate. If the parents have already devised a consistent method of communication, use it. If it is not consistent, begin establishing a reliable communication pattern. The teacher, parent, and speech therapist have to work closely with the child to establish a *yes* and *no* response. Examples of *yes* and *no* responses may be: a sound for *yes,* shaking the head for *no;* smiling for *yes,* frowning for *no;* or raising some part of the arm or hand for *yes,* no movement for *no.* Even though the teacher wants to teach the child to point, a *yes* or *no* response is essential for times when the child is away from a communication board. Establishing a way for the child to point is the next step. Some children can learn to point with a finger, others may have to use their fist. The proper placement of the material should be determined by the teacher. Some children need it up and to one side instead of in front of them. Some children can only point up and down and some only across. Eventually the teacher will want the child to achieve both. If the child has to use all his energy concentrating on his motor control, he will not be able to concentrate on the material. Thus, finding the easiest method for the child to respond is an essential step in establishing communication.

A few children emit a *yes* and *no* response with eye movements. When this method is employed, the material must be placed on a teaching device large enough for the teacher to distinguish the direction of the eye movement.

Some of the following are teaching techniques that may be used to teach reading to the severely involved athetoid or the spastic with perceptual problems.

First, teach vocabulary with real objects. Use the visual, oral, and kinesthetic approach. The child must be helped to feel shapes and textures, using both hands. Action words should be demonstrated. How can a crippled child know what hop or skip is unless he is shown? He needs to be placed on the floor to know what looking up means, and he needs to know what it feels like to use certain parts of his body even if he cannot use them by himself.

The second step is to transfer from pictures to words. Teach vocabulary by coordinating a picture vocabulary with the vocabulary in the school textbooks. The pictures can be placed on 3 × 5-inch cards and mounted on a board for the child's lesson each day. Pictures for most vocabulary words up through the fifth grade can be found in magazines. This also promotes more independent work for the child. When this reading instruction seems successful, transfer to the abstract word. Always use a lot of oral reinforcement with new abstract symbols.

More reinforcement of vocabulary can be obtained by helping the child write the word. His hand may have to be guided, but it is arm movement that makes this experience more meaningful for the child. Tracing sand and glue letters or sand paper letters with the finger is also an additional teaching aid.

Last of all, the reading material may be placed in an opaque or overhead projector. The teacher may use a pointer to teach proper eye movement. Many quadriplegics have strabismus or jerky eye movements and have to be guided for many years. Later, a strip of cardboard can be used to underline the sentence in the book. Once again, proper positioning of the book is essential to accommodate each child's discrepancies.

The severely involved child should be placed on a communication board as soon as possible: There are two types. One is for very restricted arm movements. It is usually divided into four columns with nouns, pronouns, verbs, and sometimes adjectives. This will establish a child's needs and wants quickly (Fig. 1).

TEACHER	I	AM	TIRED
MOTHER	ME	ARE	HUNGRY
FATHER	IT	IS	SLEEPY
FRIEND	YOU	WAS	HAPPY
CHILD	HE	WERE	SICK
	SHE	WANT	HURT
	THEY	NEED	THIRSTY

Figure 1.

The more involved type of communication board is made like an enlarged typewriter keyboard. The child learns to spell and make sentences on this communication board. The size of the letters depends on his hand usage and control. Hopefully, it can be decreased each year until the child can use a typewriter. Extremely involved children or those with artificial limbs may have to use a headpiece or mallet with which to strike.

Testing

The teaching of the quadriplegic is not an easy task by any means, but it is so essential for the child to be able to express himself. This means of expression may help alleviate some of the tremendous frustration this child may be experiencing through the inability to communicate with others. This established method of communication is paramount in developing his educational curriculum.

Testing the quadriplegic is a very important phase of the teaching process. The Peabody Picture Vocabulary and Ammons (for older children) tests can be adapted for pointing for *yes* and *no* answers, without interfering with their validity. Classroom inventories for color, math facts, and word knowledge can also be made to test children without usable hand use. Even the digit span can be tested. The Metropolitan is one of the easiest achievement tests to enlarge and adapt. As the child becomes older, he can be taught to transpose and answer from letter choices. If the child has poor vision or a peripheral vision loss, the reading material can be enlarged on the opaque or overhead projector.

One of the main points in testing an athetoid cerebral-palsied child is relaxation. It is wise to have a few warm-up tries before the actual testing begins. Until s/he relaxes, his/her movements will be uncontrollable. Stabilizing his/her other arm and foot also facilitates testing.

There are some testing procedures that may be utilized and adapted in order to help establish a child's strengths and weaknesses. However, there is a tremendous need for more accurate testing resources for the orthopedically handicapped child.

In concluding the area on reading instruction, the author has found that the aforementioned methods are all adaptable and relatively productive in teaching the orthopedically handicapped child. Some of the adaptations discussed in this section may be utilized in teaching any subject matter.

English

The process of teaching English to the orthopedically handicapped child is much like that of teaching reading. There are numerous adaptations to the curriculum in order to effectively teach each type of handicapped child. Individualization is again mandatory in order to meet the diverse levels of each child.

As a teacher of special children, the author is dedicated to the belief that each child is a unique individual with his own special needs and desires, as well as his own rate and style of learning. One unique and interesting method of applying individualization is through the use of learning centers. Following are a few ideas about developing a learning center for the orthopedically handicapped child.

Interest Centers

Interest centers should be an enjoyable and fun learning process for the child. In order to achieve this atmosphere, the teacher must consider the materials and surroundings with which the child will work.

Many orthopedically handicapped children have the tendency to drool; therefore, the composition of the materials should be waterproof. If paper is used, it should be laminated or covered with clear Contact® paper. This also allows the child to mark directly on the material with a grease pencil or dark crayon. It is then easily erased and ready for the next child. Other materials in the learning center should be made out of rubber or plastic if possible. The child will perform better at whatever he is doing if he does not have to be constantly aware of his drooling problem.

Durability of the materials is another important facet of learning centers. Many extremely involved athetoid or spastic cerebral-palsied children may have little or no control over their upper extremities. Therefore, if possible, materials in the learning center should be very durable or nonbreakable. Here again, the child will enjoy the learning center more if he does not have to be concerned about the possibility of destroying something.

The location of the learning center in the classroom is very vital to its success. Some handicapped children may be in wheelchairs and others may have crutches, braces, and various means of orthopedic support. The area in and around the learning center must be safely accessible to these students.

In furnishing the learning center, it is important to consider safety and comfort. Those children in wheelchairs will need tables that are easy to roll up to and adjusted to the correct height. Children with braces and crutches need sturdy chairs easy to get in and out of. For those students required to stand at specific times, standing tables need to be included. All of the above features are extremely important when planning a learning center for the orthopedically handicapped classroom.

Learning centers are very adaptable in teaching English to a class of orthopedically handicapped children. The author has found that many children need more direction than others, and still many are able to work in an independent fashion. Many paraplegics and children with muscular and bone disorders are able to function very well on their own at a learning center. This gives the teacher a chance to do more individualization with the quadri– and hemiplegic and other children who may require more specialized instruction.

Some teaching ideas that could be employed in an English learning center follow: laminated worksheets on capitalization, punctuation, and other grammatical skills are often effective. The answers to the questions may be written on the back of the sheet, so that the child may be able to see immediate results. Games involving syno–, anto–, and homonyms are sometimes fun for the child. All of these activities are primarily applicable to the paraplegic and children with muscular and bone disorders.

The quadri– and hemiplegic, who may have difficulty in writing, should be given the chance to work with activities that do not require writing skills. Materials that can be answered by matching yarn or using clothespins may be a more rewarding and fun experience for these children. Uncompleted stories that require the child to furnish an ending are very effective for language development. This activity is easily adaptable for those children who must use typewriters as a tool for writing.

The availability of ideas to be used in a learning center depends upon the teacher's own disgression and creativity. Preplanning on the teacher's part is vital in implementing a learning center in the classroom. Different teachers may use learning centers in different ways to achieve a variety of goals.

Spelling

After years of observing the teaching of physically handicapped children, the author has found that spelling can be taught in a variety of ways. The method used in teaching this subject again depends upon the physical and mental capabilities of each individual child. The following suggestions may be useful in planning and setting up an effective spelling program.

Spelling Textbooks

Paraplegics and children with muscular and bone disorders do not require many adaptive methods to the spelling program, providing they already have an established means of communication. They are issued a spelling textbook appropriate for their grade level at the beginning of the year. The children should be prepared to read and follow the directions and to work independently when they receive their spelling books. Being able to proceed through the books independently gives the child a chance to experience a great deal of success.

As the child completes a unit, he will be tested on that material. The test may be on tape in order for the child to continue working by himself. When taping a spelling test, the teacher must speak slowly and distinctly. Give the number and word, use the word in a sentence, and then repeat the word. Clear and correct pronunciation is vital, in order to avoid confusion resulting from words that sound alike. Allow sufficient time for the child to write the word before proceeding. The unit test may also be followed by dictation or other related exercises.

Using this method of teaching spelling allows the teacher time to devote more individualization to those handicapped children who are unable to work independently.

Method of Established Communication

Spelling instruction for the severely involved child is basically the same as the instruction of reading. A method of established communication is again essential in this learning process. A communication board is an effective means of instruction. Three spelling words may be written on the board in a multiple-choice fashion, with two of the spelling words misspelled. The teacher must again remember to put the board in the correct place for the child to point. The object of the lesson is for the child to be able to visually recognize the correct spelling word and point to it in a definite manner.

A child with some upper-extremity involvement who uses a typewriter should be able to complete the daily spelling lessons from the textbook. At the end of the unit, the teacher of another student may dictate the spelling words to this child.

Many orthopedically handicapped children have associated learning disabilities and perceptual problems. For this child, it is important for the teacher to determine the child's learning rate for new spelling words.

When introducing a new spelling word, the following steps should be followed:

1. Write the word (or words) on the chalkboard.
2. Teach the correct pronunciation.
3. Emphasize word meaning.
4. Use the word (or words) in oral sentences.
5. Use the following cover-write method for intensive study:
   a. Write the word three times while looking at it.
   b. Cover the word and write it.
   c. Check the word.
   d. Write the word three more times while looking at it.
   e. As the child writes the word, allow him to say it softly to himself.
6. Make sure the child has an opportunity to use words he has learned in meaningful written communication.

The above is a systematic, multisensory approach to the teaching of spelling (Love, 1968). The use of this approach in teaching spelling is more effective in teaching the learning-disabled child. As has been stated previously, learning disabilities and perceptual problems may be associated with spina bifida, victims of strokes, and cerebral-palsied children.

Spelling is a necessary tool in the orthopedically handicapped child's curriculum. This subject gives the child a chance to explore new avenues of communication. This subject should be closely related with all other subjects to enable maximum learning in for the child.

Writing Skills

Gross-motor development is a prerequisite for developing writing skills. Developing gross-motor coordination in the very early years is of the utmost importance. Before any formal writing skills can be developed, many activities need to be incorporated into the child's program.

Love (1968) states that writing skills are developed in a sequence. According to the sequence developed at the Jeane Anthony Schools in Little Rock, Arkansas, they are first developed in the air, then at the chalkboard, and then transferred to paper. After circular movements made in specific directions have been mastered by the child, the chalkboard activities are initiated. All the vertical, horizontal, and slanted lines are developed in the same manner.

Hand-eye coordination is a problem for many orthopedically handicapped children, either from poor motor control or perceptual problems. Hand-eye coordination can be promoted by a variety of means. Frostig materials, bead stringing, pegboard activities, and puzzles can be employed. Large pegs and pegboards that can be ordered from school supply companies are more beneficial for some children with serious gross-motor problems. These children may have more success at these materials if they are placed on the floor. This helps keep the materials within their reach. Some children also need larger beads and stiffer cording.

Fun activities to develop hand-eye coordination can also be employed. The following bean bag game is a good example. A string is attached to the bean bag and the child. After the child aims at a specific target and throws the bean bag, he can then pull it back with the string. This creates a fun, independent activity for the child.

The next step in the writing sequence is to develop fine-motor coordination. This can be developed by involving the child in activities of left-to-right sequencing, pegboards, beads, tracing, cutting, coloring, tearing, stencils, and using the template.

Tracing can be introduced through several techniques. A few examples would be the following: with hand and finger on oil cloth, plastic, or paper; with fingers in a box of wet or dry sand; with sand or sandpaper letters; with fingers on the chalkboard; with rhythmical strokes in the air. Tracing aids in establishing a thought pattern of writing in the child's head.

Often when using stencils, the template may need to be taped to the writing surface. If colors are used in this activity, the author has found that plastic crayons are more durable and not as likely to break as waxed crayons.

Cutting activities are often more difficult for some physically handicapped children with upper-extremity involvement. This is also especially difficult for children who have lost the use of one hand or arm due to a stroke. Some type of holding device may be helpful for the child to develop cutting skills. Four-handled scissors are also available to order. By using these, the teacher may assist the child in guiding his cutting exercises.

The next step is the development of formal writing skills. Many orthopedically handicapped children will not be able to progress this far, but for the ones that do, the teacher should begin teaching the construction of the letters in the alphabet. There are several leading methods for teaching cursive and manuscript writing, but Ruth Edington of Little Rock, Arkansas, has developed an adaptive method that appears to be more suitable for many orthopedically handicapped children. The curved construction of her letters is sometimes easier for a child with motor problems.

Much consideration should be given to the proper writing tool for the orthopedically handicapped child. Some children do not need any adaptive tool for writing, but many will. There are a few adaptations that can be used for a child who cannot use a conventional writing tool.

Some orthopedically handicapped children will need a larger grasp on their writing utensil. To achieve this, a pencil can be placed through a rubber ball, a Ping-Pong® ball, a plastic golf ball, a foam-rubber hair curler, or other adaptable materials. Masking tape or rubber bands can also be wrapped around the utensil to provide a texture easier for children to grasp. It is important that the teacher works closely with the occupational therapist in acquiring the most suitable writing tool for the child. There are some adaptive writing instruments that may be purchased, but most often it is the teacher's responsibility to create the best tool for the child. Commercial utensils may be needed to help a child with no hand usage. If legible handwriting cannot be mastered by the child, he may find success in written communication through the use of a typewriter.

Securing the paper is another major consideration. Some children may need to have their paper secured in a fixed position. The paper may be taped to the desk or writing surface, clipped to a fixed surface such as a clipboard, or secured under other means. This is primarily applicable to hemiplegics and children with upper extremity involvements.

Written communication is not mandatory in achieving a self-supporting future for the child, but it is most helpful. In today's modern, technical society, there are machines that can be adapted to most any physical disability. However, the expense involved prevents many from being able to utilize these measures. Teachers, in general, say that most children want to achieve some measure of writing success. All children may not be able to progress to the final stages of formal writing skills, but any measure of success achieved contributes to their overall coordination and development.

Social Studies Program

Teachers of orthopedically handicapped children are faced with the realization that many of their students may never have the opportunity to explore the environment of the world about them. Due to their physical handicaps, these children are often deprived of many developmental experiences that most normal children are exposed to. Social studies is, therefore, a necessity in the early childhood curriculum for the orthopedically handicapped child.

There are many resources available that compliment a social

studies program. Field trips are most effective and also school textbooks, audiovisual materials, and community speakers are viable components.

School-oriented field trips can be quite an educational experience for orthopedically handicapped children. Many of these children would not be able to attend local places of interest if it were not for special planned classroom activities. Organizing a field trip for physically handicapped children involves much thought and planning. These are some important steps to consider. The teacher should visit the place before taking the children to determine the following:

1. Are there any steps?
2. How close are the toilet facilities?
3. Can wheelchairs be pushed in the area?
4. Can the area be explored by children on crutches?
5. For an all day trip, are there facilities where the children can eat lunch?
6. For an outdoor outing: Is there a place for the children to take shelter in case of rain?

These are only a few of the many necessary arrangements to be made. Some other considerations are arranging proper transportation, packing extra clothes in case of accidents, and including correct phone numbers of parents in case of emergencies.

Field trips should be an exciting and educational experience for all the children. Some will gain more knowledge than others, but by following the aforementioned procedures, the field trip can be a safe, enriching, and rewarding experience for all those involved.

In using school textbooks, adaptive measures need to be developed in teaching the severely involved child. However, audiovisual materials and community speakers may be developed into social studies lessons enjoyed by the whole class.

Schattner (1971) believes lack of sensory stimulation and poor experiential backgrounds are often associated with the orthopedically handicapped child. Social studies is one avenue of learning that gives this type child an opportunity to explore and interpret his environment.

TEACHING MATHEMATICS

Often math can be taught to the handicapped child in basically the same manner as instruction for the nonhandicapped child. Once again, the previous mentioned adaptations will have to be utilized in the instruction of math. Examples are tearing workbooks apart for students who use typewriters, providing necessary tools for the child to hold his materials, and establishing a means of either written or oral communication.

Individualization

Some of the math instruction for the handicapped child has to be individualized to accommodate each child's special problems. Writing an objectives chart for each child at the beginning of the year is a valuable tool in establishing their math curriculum. Rarely will each child be working on the same objective simultaneously. Objectives for each child are based on his understanding of mathematics as determined by diagnostic tests and other procedures. Once objectives are selected, a teacher must help a child choose appropriate ways to accomplish them. It is essential to begin with a well-organized program.

Math should be taught like reading. Initially, the teacher should begin with real objects and advance to abstract symbols.

Methods

Stamp Pads, Abacus

There are many different methods that can be used to instill math concepts even for a child with poor fine motor coordination. Stamp pads are immediate positive reinforcement in visualizing number values. For example, a child could look at the number 6 and stamp six shapes to promote number understanding. In using any kind of blocks as concrete objects to establish number concepts, the materials should be restricted by a retainer. This prevents the child from constantly knocking blocks or materials out of his reach. An abacus or other counting instruments may require fixation for children with upper extremity involvement. Any special adaptive techniques that will reinforce number concepts and number facts are most beneficial. After a sound mathematics foundation is established, more abstract concepts will follow.

Communication Board

The communication board is also a valuable device in teaching the severely involved child. The numbers 1 through 10 are placed at the top, and 20, 30, 40, 50, 60, 70, 80, 90, and 100 are below. The signs for the processes are arranged at the sides so the child can indicate the process to be used (Fig. 2). As the child advances, signs for carrying, borrowing, fractions, division, and other processes can be added. Most children without hand use will have to do more math in their heads, since they will be without the manual dexterity to use learning crutches. This makes math one of the hardest subjects to teach them. If they can learn to add columns by making ten combinations, it will probably be the biggest achievement in their mastery of math.

+									X
1	2	3	4	5	6	7	8	9	10
	20	30	40	50	60	70	80	90	100
−									÷

Figure 2.

Group Instruction

Some mathematical concepts in the classroom can be taught as group instruction. For many teachers, group experiences have been found to be very valuable. For example, these concepts can be taught as units: telling time, fractions, calendar skills, measurements, and monetary values. In classroom experiences, even though students are not working on the same academic level, adapted units can meet each child's individual instructional level. Some students will progress further than others, but it can be a meaningful and learning experience for each child.

Understanding

Kennedy and Michon (1973) indicate that a child's understanding begins as he manipulates concrete materials, grows as he works with representations of objects and ideas, and matures when he grasps the abstract concepts that come from earlier work. Attempts to shortcut the process by having children work at an abstract level without benefit of earlier concrete and representational work are almost certainly doomed to failure. He must manipulate objects, not merely watch others do it. He must learn to question, reason, and discover patterns as he refines his understanding of concepts and processes. Then he must form his own generalizations about the ideas with which he has been dealing. It is the instructor's responsibility to help each child achieve these objectives.

Summary

Developing a language arts and math curriculum for the orthopedically handicapped child must revolve around a positive educational environment allowing the child to achieve his maximum level of functioning in all areas of learning.

The educational goals of the orthopedically handicapped child are basically the same as for all school children. Some handicapped children have disabilities that can be "lived with" in a relatively normal fashion, while others are so deviant that educational goals for them must be very different. The achievement of these goals relies upon the alternative strategies and adaptive measures employed by the teacher of the orthopedically handicapped child.

Language arts and math constitute a major portion of the educational curriculum of the orthopedically handicapped child.

Modification of the goals set for these specific areas will vary depending on the child's needs and educational progress. As I have stated in this chapter, the use of many special provisions can successfully eliminate the need for specialized instruction.

The proper educational objective for each orthopedically handicapped child in the areas of language arts and math should be based on a program where each child has the opportunity to work at his/her own level, in his/her preferred way, progressing as far and as fast as his learning capacities permit. Whether dealing with the lowest- or highest-functioning handicapped child, the educator's responsibility is to develop in every human being his uppermost potentials and capabilities.

REFERENCES

Hammill, D.D. and Myers, P.I.: *Methods for Learning Disorders.* New York, JW, 1969.

Kennedy, L.M. and Michon, R.L.: *Games for Individualizing Mathematics.* Columbus, Merrill 1973.

Love, H.D.: *Teaching the Educable Mentally Retarded.* Berkeley, McCutchan, 1968.

Schattner, R.: *An Early Child Curriculum for Multiply Handicapped Children.* New York, John Day, 1971.

Chapter 5

TEACHING CEREBRAL-PALSIED CHILDREN

Definition and Incidence

CEREBRAL PALSY is a general term Deaver (1967, p. 3) defines as "neuromuscular disability caused by lesions in the motor centers of the brain—before birth, at birth, or during infancy and childhood."

The brain is the center of muscular control, and the resulting disturbances of motor function may include incoordination, weakness, paralysis, spasticity, athetosis, rigidity, and/or tremors. Keats (1965, p. 9) states that the brain damage may not only produce a neuromuscular dysfunction, but it may also cause mental deficiency, personality and behavior problems, sensory defects, and convulsions, "depending on the location of the lesion and degree of involvement."

Most authorities agree that cerebral palsy has undoubtedly existed since the beginning of recorded history. Love (1972) discusses the biblical descriptions of lame persons and heiroglyphics in ancient Egypt that illustrate the characteristic postures of those afflicted with cerebral palsy. William John Little published a monograph in 1862, describing what is now known as cerebral palsy; he told of the spastic, drooling, and grimacing child with the scissors gait. This description gave the erroneous impression that all youngsters with cerebral palsy were of that type and affected mentally. As Deaver (1967) explains, impaired intelligence does not always accompany cerebral palsy, and spasticity is present in only one particular type of the disorder, so the term Little's disease does not appropriately describe all those with cerebral palsy. Kirk (1962) gives credit to Doctor Winthrop Phelps for coining of the term *cerebral palsy.*

The figures and studies concerning the incidence of cerebral palsy seem to differ somewhat, but the majority of available information seems to indicate that economic, geographic or social factors do not affect the incidence. Cousins, Hopkins and Phelps (1958) believe that 7 children per 100,000 of the general population are born with the disorder. One of seven of the children dies before six years of age, and there are about 275,000 cerebral-palsied persons under the age of twenty-one (Cousins et al., 1958).

Causes of Cerebral Palsy

The major causes of cerebral palsy may be divided into three main categories: (1) prenatal causes (before birth), (2) natal or perinatal (during birth), and (3) postnatal (after birth).

Kirk (1962, p. 358) states that the prenatal causes of cerebral palsy include genetic or inherited conditions and also "conditions during pregnancy which result in a defect in the child's central nervous system." Cousins et al. (1958) believe that cerebral palsy is rarely inherited, and that 30 to 40 percent of cerebral palsy cases are caused by developmental defects occurring before birth. In the prenatal category, Marks (1974) includes the following factors: congenital factors (rubella, for example) or other maternal infections, such as influenza, measles, mumps; the Rh factor; and maternal metabolic diseases. Concerning prenatal causes, Kirk (1962) cites these factors: severe anemia in the mother, shock, anoxia, a serious heart condition, and threatened abortion.

The second category of causes of cerebral palsy (natal) is from the onset of labor until the child's birth. Deaver (1967) lists eight basic natal causes as follows:

1. Anoxia—due to difficulties with the cord and placenta
2. Asphyxia—caused by blockage of the respiratory passages
3. Analgesics—affecting the respiratory center of the infant
4. Trauma—injuring the brain during difficult or prolonged labor or by a too strenuous application of forceps
5. Breech birth—may cause the time between the delivery of the head to be a potential period of anoxia
6. Sudden changes in pressure—both spontaneous deliveries and caesarean sections may result in a sudden release of pressure and cause hemorrhage and ruptured blood vessels
7. Prematurity—premature infant is more likely to suffer from

cerebral hemorrhage, due to his thinner and weaker blood vessels and blood vessel walls
8. Vitamin K—a lack of this vitamin in the child may cause a tendency to bleed. This is responsible for a very small amount of cerebral palsy cases and can often be corrected by giving vitamin K to the mother while she is in labor.

The third category of causes (postnatal) occurs after birth. In this category, Brashear, Raney, and Shands (1971) include the following: vascular, infectious, or traumatic lesions (such as those of meningitis) ; encephalitis; vascular accidents; anoxia; and also Rh incompatibility associated with jaundice of the newborn.

Topographical Classification
Monoplegia is the term used when a single limb is involved (which is rather rare) ; *hemiplegia* refers to the involvement of both limbs on the same side of the body. When both lower limbs are involved, the term *paraplegia* is appropriate, and when involvement of all four limbs is indicated, *quadriplegia* is the term used. *Spastic diplegia* is frequently used to denote bilateral involvement in which spastic paralysis affects the lower much more than the upper limbs (Brasher, et al., 1971). Love (1972) points out that in the case of paraplegics and hemiplegics, cerebral palsy is usually the spastic type, whereas the quadriplegic may be athetoid, rigid, or spastic.

Physiological Classification
In physiological classification of the cerebral palsied, Love (1972) refers to the following three types: (1) *spasticity;* (2) *dyskinesia,* including athetosis, tremor, and rigidity; and (3) *ataxia.*

Spasticity accounts for approximately 60 percent of all cerebral palsy cases, and as H. B. Robinson and N. Robinson (1965, p. 168) state, these children have "one or more limbs which are rigidly immobilized by constant muscular contractions." A spastic child's motions may be fairly accurate, but he makes them slowly and with a great amount of effort. He may often sit most of the time and be unable to enunciate properly. As Denhoff and Robinault (1960) state, to make a diagnosis of spasticity, the pathologic stretch reflex must be present. Denhoff and Robinault (1960) also feel that spasticity is characterized by an enlarged reflexogenic area, ankle clonus, and an abnormal synchronization of the discharge rate in different parts of the spastic muscle. Kirk (1962, p. 355) reports that the balance between the suppressors and antagonistic muscles is absent, and, as a result, there are "jerky, uncontrolled movements with the spasmodic contraction of the muscles."

Athetosis, rigidity, and tremor types of cerebral palsy are often included in the dyskinesia category. According to H. B. Robinson, and N. Robinson (1965, p. 169), the term *dyskinesia* refers to "abnormalities in the amount and type of motor activities." As Love (1972, p. 136) points out, this abnormality in motion may be "slow or rapid, constant or intermittent."

Athetosis is the second most common type of cerebral palsy (about 20% of the total) and is characterized by uncontrollable, irregular, and jerky movements. Children with athetosis walk in a stumbly and lurching manner, and their heads are frequently drawn back, mouths held open, tongues protruding, and drooling occurs. As Kirk (1962) points out, though, during sleep the involuntary movements seem to disappear.

Tremor and rigidity occur in only a small percentage of cerebral-palsied children. Tremor cerebral palsy is evident when the entire body shows irregular, involuntary, vibrating movements. Kirk (1962, p. 356) feels that the child affected with this type of cerebral palsy is usually predictable and fairly consistent and can "direct his activities toward a goal more adequately than the athetoid or spastic." The children affected with rigidity are slow moving and have trouble extending their limbs fully due to almost constant partial contraction.

The third major physiological classification of cerebral palsy is *ataxia* (which accounts for about 8% of the total) and is characterized by a disturbance of balance and equilibrium. Deaver (1967, p. 11) states that the pathological lesion is due to the "involvement of the cerebellum and its tracts." Ataxic children may be quite flexible, but due to a lack of balance, they may not walk nearly as soon as normal youngsters. Cousins et al. (1958) believe the ataxic child has the best chance for complete recovery among all the cerebral-palsied groups although the outlook is obviously better for the child who is not further handicapped with epilepsy or mental retardation.

Intelligence

Kirk (1962, p. 359) seems to feel that "there is actually little direct relation between intelligence and degree of physical impairment in cerebral palsy." It is difficult to accurately assess a cerebral-palsied child's intelligence quotient, because of low scores on performance test items (particularly if the subject is severely affected). McDonald and Chance (1962) report that only about 25 percent of children suffering from cerebral palsy may be classified as normal or above normal, and about 30 percent are slightly mentally retarded.

Classification According to Severity

Deaver (1967, p. 12) bases his classification according to severity on "the patient's ability to perform the activities of daily living." According to Deaver (1967, p. 12), a person who is only mildly affected with cerebral palsy "is able to care for his daily needs and ambulates without the aid of any appliances." He defines a moderately affected individual as the one who "needs special types of treatment as he is inadequate in self-care, ambulation and/or speech" and the severely affected as the patient who "needs treatment but the degree of involvement is so severe that prognosis for self-care, ambulation and speech is very poor."

Educational Alternatives and Considerations

Multiple handicaps are usually associated with cerebral palsy, and as a result, the education of those children affected is a complex and involved problem. A cerebral-palsied child's main handicap may involve the neuromuscular system, but as Deaver (1967, p. 55) states, "80% of these children have speech difficulties, 70% are mentally retarded, 65% are left handed, 50% have visual difficulties, 40% of the spastic type have sensory loss, about 8% have hearing loss and any or all of these conditions may be associated with seizures and personality problems."

Education is much more than simply attending school or working up to one's academic potential. It should also include the development of attitudes, habits, self-help skills, and positive self-concepts; this is especially true for the education of cerebral-palsied children. If at all possible, a cerebral-palsied child should attend both nursery school and kindergarten. Providing that the nursery school personnel show a knowledge of the special needs of cerebral-palsied children, Hatton (1962) believes the nursery school can provide opportunities for specialized remedial work which may improve the frequent perceptual problems of these handicapped children.

When the time comes for a cerebral-palsied child to enter school, parents must discuss and evaluate the educational alternatives available in their community and determine which will best meet the needs of the child. Cousins et al. (1958, p. 146) feel that the "degree of physical impairment is the most important criterion in determining proper placement of a brain-injured child." In many instances, the parents must choose between sending their child to regular classes in a public school, to special classes in a public school, or to a special school for handicapped children. School placements should depend on whether the child's physical and educational handicaps are severe or mild and which handicap (either physical or educational) is the more severe. It is extremely important, of course, that the parents evaluate their child's handicaps in an honest and realistic manner. As Cruickshank (1955) points out, the educational program for these children will be at least partially dictated by those who are enrolled—including methods, materials, and class size. Cruickshank (1955) further states that one teacher cannot effectively handle more than ten students, and chronological age-range (within one group) should not be more than four years. Most of the time, it is necessary for the teacher to work with the students on a one-to-one basis or in very small groups, because individual differences among cerebral-palsied children are so extreme.

Associated Problems and Their Educational Implications

Speech

According to Brown, Curtis, Edney, Johnson, and Keaster (1948) as many as 70 percent of all cerebral-palsied children have speech problems. It would appear obvious that cerebral-palsied children usually have delayed speech development. Besides neuromuscular problems, cerebral-palsied children often have hearing, visual, intellectual, perceptual, and behavioral problems that may interfere with normal speech development (Johnson et al., 1948). Frequently, the cerebral-palsied child may exhibit faulty articulation patterns, a monotonous and breathy voice, and irregular and effortful speech. L. Gurren, I.W. Karlin, and D.B. Karlin (1965) state that the athetoid type has the largest incidence of speech defects. Contrary to the athetoid, though, Gurren et al. (1965, p. 264) feel that the "spastic may be limited in the direction and extent of movement or the speech organs, but his control is not impaired," while the ataxic "has little awareness as to whether he has made the appropriate response."

If a speech therapist is available in the school system, the classroom teacher should assist him by giving information concerning how well and how much the student talks in class. The teacher should also make special considerations with regard to oral assignments, seating arrangements, and specific classroom tasks and duties.

Johnson et al. (1948) feel that relaxation may be one of the students' main problems, and that it would be beneficial for the teacher to organize the classroom routine in a way to provide for frequent periods of rest and relaxation. Unfortunately, some cerebral-palsied children are not included in daily conversations at home or family discussions, and the teacher should encourage the child to notice things in his environment, using all his senses. It may be necessary to imitate everyday sounds to try to see if the child comprehends or to encourage the child to actually imitate the sounds.

The teacher should praise the child for any effort s/he makes, even if it is only an unintelligible sound, and make a sincere effort not to always anticipate his needs and answer for him; it is much more beneficial for the child to try to convey his own desires. The child's classmates and his teacher should remember to be good listeners, even though what the child may be expressing is simply jibberish. Keats (1965, p. 199) states it is important to remember that it is "through speech, expressive or receptive behavior, that the child will reveal his intelligence, personality and his character more accurately than through any other mode of expression."

Hearing

Hearing defects are frequently associated handicaps of the cerebral palsied. Keats (1965) feels that the cerebral-palsied child most affected with the problem is the athetoid with a background of kernicterus, but that it is important for all cerebral-palsied children to have their hearing tested early in childhood. According to Kirk (1965), hearing losses (especially among athetoids) are not as common as visual defects but, of course, are still an important consideration in the education of cerebral palsied children.

Three specific therapeutic measures for children with hearing problems are discussed by Gurren et al. (1965, p. 273) : "first, training in speech development; second, auditory training; third, speech reading." The classroom teacher may be helpful in the area of auditory training, if he allows the child to make the best use of any residual hearing. This goal may be realized through training the student to listen, to discriminate more selectively, and to adjust to possible methods of amplification such as hearing aids (Gurren et al., 1965). Most children will need assurance and encouragement from classmates and teachers, so they can adjust to hearing aids more efficiently and quickly. The seating arrangement is a very important factor to be considered by the teacher so that the child will not be unnecessarily frustrated or embarrassed.

Vision

The incidence of visual defects in cerebral-palsied persons seems to differ, but it is apparent that such defects are common. Usually these neurological abnormalities, according to Keats (1965), are directly related to the cerebral pathology and include defective eye movements, impaired vision, field-of-vision difficulties, and blindness. It is apparent to Keats (1965, p. 275) that defective eye movements in the cerebral palsied child may not affect total body movement, and in most children, "the eye movements seem to improve with increased control of the involuntary motion of the extremities." Cousins et al. (1958) believe that the inability to control eye muscles is associated with Rh incompatibility and limits the vertical motions of the eye to the extent that the child finds it necessary to move his head instead of his eyes. Nystagmus may cause the ataxic child's eyes to move almost constantly and interfere with clear vision. Fortunately, this particular condition can be partially alleviated through proper treatment.

For the classroom teacher (and all involved personnel) of cerebral-palsied children, visual handicaps should definitely be considered in daily routines and educational materials. When the child is performing a specific task, the teacher should observe how he is holding his head and how he is actually looking at the specific object. In very severe cases of impaired vision due to cerebral disorientation, Woods (1957) reports that these children may not be able to comprehend the three dimensions of every day life, and, in extremely severe instances, these children may not recognize objects at all.

Perception

Associated with visual problems are perceptual difficulties, also very common in cerebral-palsied children, although as Bice, Cruickshank, Lynch, and Wallen (1957) point out, additional research is needed to more accurately determine the extent, incidence, and treatment of the various types of perceptual disorders. Bice et al. (1957, p. 21) support the view that brain injury is associated with "impaired performance on various sorts of perceptual tasks in both the visual and tactual areas." According to Keats (1965), auditory perception defects are usually diagnosed fairly early in life, since it is obvious to the parent that something is definitely wrong when the child does not respond to the spoken word. The parents will often then seek professional help and may be informed that their child has either expressive or receptive aphasia or a speech problem of central nervous system origin and should inform the teacher of any test results.

The educational considerations concerning perceptual problems are numerous and diversified. Some cerebral-palsied children have a loss of depth perception and may not be able to walk up stairs very easily or accurately judge the height of a curb. The teacher should be alert to these problems and try to avoid or at least anticipate possible situations which may be troublesome in new and unfamiliar environments. Foreground-background confusions appear in many cerebral-palsied children, and as Keats (1965, p. 317) states it, these children "know all about a button and nothing about the dress on which they see it." This type of perceptual disorder may explain why some cerebral-palsied children have difficulty tying their shoes. Holt (1965) states that this problem may be due to the inability to distinguish a black shoelace against a black shoe.

Sheeran (1965) feels that the difficult aspects of mathematics for the cerebral palsied are geometry and trigonometry, especially if the student has defects in spatial perception. According to Sheeran (1965), many pupils who can distinguish two separate triangles cannot distinguish them if they overlap, and he recommends using colored chalk. In order for a child with special perception problems to fully comprehend a three-dimensional figure, it would seem to be advisable to use solid models.

Denhoff and Robinault (1960) believe it is helpful to the child with perceptual problems to have the teacher simplify elements involved in a specific task; emphasize items that can be rather easily discriminated by color, size, or texture; and make allowances when the handicap is severe. For example, a child who recognizes a letter but cannot write it should be allowed to use a typewriter.

Perceptual disorders may make the performance of simple tasks very difficult and frustrating for the cerebral palsied. This should be understood by the teacher with regard to the child's brushing hair or teeth or dressing, etc. The instructor should be sure that the child knows the position of various body parts and that he is aware of the correct orientation of objects he is using (Holt, 1968, p. 188). Self-help skills are extremely difficult to master, if the child does not know when his clothes are inside out or upside down.

Teachers of the cerebral palsied should take note of the perceptual problems discussed by Woods (1957) and help each child accordingly: difficulties in translating three dimensions of ordinary vision into two dimensions of pictures, problems in distinguishing left and right and up and down or round shapes from square, and inabilities to recognize letters or identify specific objects in pictures.

When teaching arithmetic, the teacher should realize that some cerebral-palsied children may have no idea of number values. They may not be able to say that five is less than six or even give the correct number of objects (pegs, for example) when asked to do so (Woods, 1957). This inability to deal with simple mathematics (Woods feels) may coexist with an ability to read and write at an average level for the child. Woods (1957) also points out that those children who demonstrate severe arithmetic problems may show signs of Gerstmann's syndrome (when a hand is covered, they are unable to identify which finger is being touched) or their problems may more importantly be due to difficulties in consecutive thought or perseveration.

Drawings done by cerebral-palsied children may show such disorientation as inaccurate proportions and an emphasis on unessential detail. When involving a child in an art activity, the teacher should praise him frequently and encourage his effort—regardless of the quality of the project.

A person teaching cerebral-palsied children with perceptual problems would benefit from conferring with a learning disabilities teacher concerning specific remedial activities. The teacher of cerebral palsied children should not overlook each student's physical limitations, though, and evaluate each activity accordingly. Lerner (1971) gives the following list of activities for remediation of visual, auditory, haptic, and cross-model perception problems: (1) Visual perception activities might include reproducing pegboard or block designs, finding particular shapes in pictures, classifying and matching geometric shapes, finding missing parts in a picture, or assembling puzzles. (2) Auditory perception activities include discriminations of sounds that are loud and soft, high and low, etc., improving sensitivity to sounds, attending for sound patterns, and developing an awareness of letter sounds. (3) Activities in the haptic perception group may involve feeling various textures, shapes, and weights, identifying letters by touching and arranging the different sizes of geometric shapes while blindfolded. (4) Cross-modal perception activities include having the student look at a pattern of dots and dashes and then repeating it on a drum rhythmically, asking the child to feel shapes in a box and then draw the shapes felt, and describing a picture to a student and asking him to select the picture described from several choices.

Seizures

Seizures occur quite frequently in cerebral palsied children. Cousins et al. (1958) report that, according to a New Jersey study of 1265 children, 29.2 percent had a seizure frequency or incidence. (This incidence varies with the type of cerebral palsy.) Teachers should keep records of types and severity of seizures and know when to administer medication if it becomes necessary. It should be explained to others in the classroom (if it appears necessary) what a seizure is and how to cope with it so that all those involved will be able to adjust more efficiently.

Personalities, Psychological Differences, and Emotional Behavior

When a teacher is trying to understand the cerebral-palsied child, s/he must keep in mind that the normal child is different from the handicapped in two ways as described by Bice and Cruickshank (1955, pp. 116-117): (1) The normal child "is able to communicate or freely move around in his environment and thus can affect changes in barriers to this adjustment. (2) For the normal person the barrier itself is rarely the same in all situations." The cerebral-palsied child is often unable to communicate efficiently or move about independently and directing changes in his environment is often difficult. As Bice and Cruickshank (1955) point out, the cerebral palsied is faced with the same disability in all aspects of his adjustment. In order to be a satisfied and well-adjusted individual, the cerebral-palsied person must develop a positive self-concept. The cerebral-palsied child is quite responsive to the way others act toward him and tends to be self-conscious, excitable, or distractible. As Johnson et al. (1948, p. 388) state, "an important part of the cerebral-palsied child is the development of emotional control . . . and whether and how readily he can acquire the desired emotional poise depends on the understanding and cooperation of those working with him."

Denhoff and Robinault (1960, p. 106) feel that a lack of motivation is a primary problem when working with the cerebral palsied children. They recommend that the teacher analyze children's physical, mental, and emotional needs and "supply goals sufficiently within their reach to insure a sustained drive." This appears to be a much better approach than constantly looking for gadgets to stimulate seemingly unmotivated children.

Parents often overprotect and indulge their handicapped child. When attempts are made to correct this negative behavior, the child often responds with an emotional display, and this display can easily develop into a habit. Another problem concerning the cerebral-palsied child is that some parents pay little or no attention to a child when he is behaving, so in order to gain attention, the child misbehaves (Cousins et al., 1958). Another serious emotional disturbance can develop when a child is unable to speak and makes a sincere effort to make his desires known, but he becomes frustrated and discouraged and then refuses to try to communicate any further.

When a child's goals are set too high (either by himself or his parents) it can lead to emotional problems. A teacher should be aware of such a situation and be sure that the child is directed toward progressive goals to "overcome frustrations due to lack of ability to perform a complete function" (Cousins et al., 1958, p. 109).

Even though it is a difficult job, a teacher should help the cerebral-palsied child realize his limitations and set realistic goals for himself to avoid the development of feelings of inadequacy.

These feelings of inadequacy are frequently found in mildly handicapped children more than others, since their problems are not always immediately apparent to those around them.

Severe defects in vision and hearing may cause antisocial behavior, since the child cannot observe group activities clearly or adequately and as a result, does not know what is expected of him (Cousins et al., 1958). These defects may produce feelings of insecurity and timidity.

Special Classroom Adaptations and Equipment

Working with cerebral-palsied children requires a great deal of patience and also special modifications in learning situations so the child can work to his/her potential. There are also some building modifications Osdol and Shane (1972) feel should be considered. These include building ramps, widening doors, installing handrails, and providing adequate space for physical, occupational, and speech therapy. Special eating utensils are available for those with cerebral palsy. Marks (1974) mentions various learning aids, such as sentence boards to help the child associate spoken with written words; number boards with sponge digits for those children with undependable or weak grasps; tilt-top desk-tables; lock-block boards for learning words, numbers, or letters; and several devices for turning pages. Special drawing instruments, such as compasses and rulers, are also made for the cerebral palsied. As Levin (1964) points out, it might be helpful for the child if a blackboard is placed on an easel and he practices writing patterns from a standing position before attempting more tedious tasks from a sitting position with only regular pencil and paper. Levin (1964) feels that electric typewriters are more beneficial than the manuals and help to develop finger coordination and improve a drop-wrist position.

Games for the Cerebral Palsied

It is important for cerebral-palsied children (especially those attending some type of public school) to engage in purposeful and educational physical activities. Many games suggested by Breen and Cratty (1972) would probably be taught by a physical education teacher, although some could easily be adapted for classroom use. Those persons teaching physically handicapped children such games need to keep in mind that some activities that seem apparently useful may not be at all appropriate for cerebral palsied children. For example, an instructor should not attempt to correct a cerebral-palsied child's poor balance by having him walk narrow lines or use a balance beam; "this could actually aggravate their atypical gait patterns." (Breen and Cratty, 1972, p. 12).

Several games suggested by Breen and Cratty (1972) involve manipulation of wheelchairs and improving the manner in which crutches are used. Others deal with quantitative concepts and mathematical operations, language and reading skills, and even categorization. All these proposed games can be varied and modified in many ways to suit the needs of cerebral palsied children when an interested and imaginative teacher is involved.

Therapy

Speech, occupational, and physical therapies are extremely important for children with cerebral palsy. Chance and McDonald (1964, p. 63) feel that probably "no other problem in rehabilitation places a greater obligation for accurate observing and reporting on the therapist than does the program for the cerebral palsied." It is also extremely important for the classroom teacher to work with the various therapists and offer any information concerning the child's progress in school and be familiar with the therapists' goals and procedures.

As previously mentioned, speech defects among the cerebral palsied are common, and the value of speech therapy is obvious. The classroom teacher should work with the speech therapist in determining possible activities which could be included in the everyday school routine.

It would appear beneficial for the classroom teacher to know what remedial activities for perceptual and conceptual difficulties the occupational therapist uses so he can employ similar activities in the classroom. As Denhoff and Robinault (1960) report, occupational therapists often use objects emphasizing variations in shape, texture, size, and color, and these can provide numerous possibilities for investigating perceptual problems. Occupational therapy for the cerebral palsied emphasizes the practical types of activities geared to help the child become as self-sufficient as possible (Keats, 1956).

According to Keats (1965), the physical therapy program for the cerebral palsied child must strive to reach the goals of ambulating and learning physical skills of the normal maturing child. Physical therapy is a necessary part of a comprehensive rehabilitation program. As Love (1972 p. 140) states, "physical therapy aids the cerebral palsied in achieving their total capabilities through the use of active, passive, and resistive exercises; by initiating normal joint motion patterns; and establishing balance and functional activities." It is again beneficial for the classroom teacher to be cognizant of the physical therapy techniques being employed, so any progress seen in the classroom can be encouraged and reported to the therapist.

Speech, occupational, and physical therapists must work together with other school personnel to discuss and adjust therapy schedules so that the child receives the most beneficial educational and therapeutic program.

Teacher-Parent Relationships

It is of prime importance for a teacher of cerebral-palsied children to develop a satisfying relationship with the parents. It is quite common for a teacher to feel that protective parents must be encouraged to relinquish their hold on the handicapped child, and also, the teacher's own aggression may be aroused by aggressive, militant parents (Loring and Mason, 1966). It is much easier for a teacher to sympathize with the feelings of the parent whose worry about his child is simply anxious concern than it is to realize that an angry parent is trying to show the same basic concern, only through different behavior. Teachers of cerebral-palsied children usually become familiar with the parent who is upset when his child is moved to a different class. Unfortunately, "the parents rarely see this as a move to place the child in a more suitable setting, they tend to think in terms of promotion or demotion" . . . (Loring and Mason, 1966, p. 52). As a result, the teacher may feel his judgment is being questioned and become slightly resentful. The teacher should realize, though, that the parents are simply clinging to the basic hope that their child will improve and try to help them understand their feelings.

A possible source of friction may develop between parents and teachers, if the child shows confusion concerning behavior viewed differently by parents and teachers. Another area of misunderstanding can develop when a teacher who has a good relationship with a child has helped him make progress. The teacher should try and keep in mind that, for the parents, the very fact that he has succeeded may only emphasize their own sense of failure and despair.

Parents of cerebral—palsied children have complicated and ambivalent feelings and often are unable to accept the fact that their child is indeed handicapped, which only makes the teacher's job more difficult. "It is only when parents have really accepted all the implications of the handicap that they are able to cooperate with all that the school offers" (Loring and Mason, 1966, p. 54).

Summary

Cerebral palsy is a complex neuromuscular disorder involving many associated handicaps. Those individuals teaching cerebral palsied children need patience and understanding, along with being well informed and familiar with any new educational methods or materials. In order for the education of cerebral-palsied children to be most beneficial, teachers should be able to successfully work with others in the rehabilitation program, including various therapists, social workers, physicians, and parents. The concept of individual differences is probably more meaningful in dealing with cerebral-palsied children than it is concerning children in the regular classroom. The community must do all that is possible to develop a comprehensive rehabilitation and educational program to best meet the needs of all involved cerebral-palsied children.

REFERENCES

Bice, H.V. and Cruickshank, W.M.: Personality characteristics. In Cruickshank, W.M. and Raus, G.M. (Eds.): *Cerebral Palsy—Its Individual and*

Community Problems. Syracuse, Syracuse U Pr, 1955.

Bice, H.V., Cruickshank, W.M., Lynch, K., and Wallen, N.: *Perception and Cerebral Palsy: Studies in Figure-Background Relationship*. Syracuse, Syracuse U Pr, 1957.

Brashear, R. Jr., Raney, B.R., and Shands, A.R., *Shand's Handbook of Orthopaedic Surgery*. St. Louis, Mosby, 1971.

Breen, J.E. and Cratty, B.J., *Educational Games for Physically Handicapped Children*. Denver, Love, 1972.

Brown, S.F., Curtis, J.F., Edney, C.W., Johnson, W., and Keaster, J.: *Speech Handicapped School Children*. New York, Harp–Row, 1948.

Chance, B. Jr., and McDonald, E.T.: *Cerebral Palsy*. Englewood Cliffs, P-H, 1964.

Cousins, R., Hopkins, T.W., and Phelps, W.: *The Cerebral-Palsied Child: A Guide for Parents*. New York, S, 1958.

Cruickshank, W.H.: Educational planning for the cerebral palsied. In Cruickshank, W.M. and Raus, G.M. (Eds.): *Cerebral Palsy—Its Individual and Community Problems*. Syracuse, Syracuse U Pr, 1955.

Deaver, G.G.: *Cerebral Palsy: Methods of Evaluation and Treatment*. New York, The Institute of Rehabilitation Medicine, New York University Medical Center, 1967.

Denhoff, E. and Robinault, I.: *Cerebral Palsy and Related Disorders: A Developmental Approach to Dysfunction*. New York, McGraw 1960.

Gurren, L., Karlin, D.B., and Karlin, I.W.: *Development and Disorders of Speech in Childhood*. Springfield, Thomas, 1965.

Hatton, D.A.: *Understanding Cerebral Palsy: For Parents of the Cerebral Palsied Child*. Erie, Pennsylvania, Erie County Crippled Children's Society, 1962.

Holt, K.S.: *Assessment of Cerebral Palsy*. London, Lloyd-Luke (Medical Books) Ltd., 1965.

Keats, S.: *Cerebral Palsy*. Springfield, Thomas, 1965.

Kirk, S.A.: *Educating Exceptional Children*. Boston, Houghton, 1962.

Lerner, J.W.: *Children with Learning Disabilities*. Boston, Houghton, 1971.

Levin, A.: *Cerebral Palsy: The Pioneer Years of Occupational Therapy in Scotland*. Edinburgh and London, E. and S. Livingstone Ltd., 1964.

Loring, J. and Mason, A.: *The Spastic School Child and the Outside World*. England, Spastics Society in Association with William Heinemann Ltd., 1966.

Love, H.D.: *Educating Exceptional Children in Regular Classrooms*. Springfield, Thomas, 1972.

Marks, N.C.: *Cerebral Palsied and Learning Disabled Children*. Springfield, Thomas, 1974.

Osdol, W.R.V. and Shane, D.G.: *An Introduction to Exceptional Children*. Dubuque, Iowa, Brown Pub, 1972.

Robinson H.B. and Robinson, N.: *The Mentally Retarded Child.* New York, McGraw, 1965.

Sheeran, J.L.: Problems encountered in teaching mathematics to cerebrally palsied children. In Loring, J. (Ed.): *Teaching the Cerebral Palsied Child.* England, Spastics Society in Association with William Heinemann., 1965.

Woods, G.E.: *Cerebral Palsy in Childhood.* Bristol, England, John Wright and Son, Ltd., 1957.

Chapter 6

ARCHITECTURAL BARRIERS IN THE SCHOOLS

THE HANDICAPPED child has no idea when he leaves his home whether he will be able to be an independent individual or if he will be required by architectural barriers to be dependent on other individuals. He knows that, given the right set of circumstances, he could manage alone. What he does not always know is whether that set of circumstances will be provided. Will he have to wait at a set of steps for someone to come along and help him? Will he need assistance in going to the bathroom? What a depressing experience it must be for the handicapped child when confronted with these problems over which he has no control.

With the movement toward mainstreaming, it becomes increasingly important for the local school districts to provide adequate facilities for the handicapped child. Children who were once sent to residential, day, or hospital schools will be coming to the public schools for their educational needs.

Transportation

When the problems posed for the handicapped child as s/he approaches school age are considered, a means of transporting him/her to school must be first discussed. The regular school bus is not going to satisfy the need: It calls for a specially adapted bus. This bus *should* be equipped with a hydraulic lift for lifting the wheelchair into the bus. A bus for the purpose of transporting the handicapped *should* have a portion of the seats removed, providing a space with a means of securing the chair.

An alternative to a specially equipped bus is a van with a loading ramp. This would provide a less expensive means for the school district with only a few handicapped children. The van would also need to be equipped with a means for securing the

108

wheelchairs. For parents who bring their own children, there should be reserved parking (May, Waggoner, and Hotte, 1974).

Outside the School

Walkways outside the school should be hard and smooth but not slick (Gutman and Gutman, 1968). It would be best to have broad and shallow steps for those on crutches or for the cerebral-palsied child.

A shallow ramp should be provided for those in wheelchairs. Concrete ramps may be roughened by jabbing the cement while wet with broom bristles. The grade ought not exceed 1 foot in 12 feet of length (Gutman and Gutman, 1968). For safety, the ramp ought to have at least one handrail. Two handrails would naturally be better.

It is recommended that asphalt paving be avoided, since in hot weather it softens, and wheelchairs may sink into it.

Gratings should have bars at right angles to the direction of travel to prevent the wheelchairs from slipping between the bars. Covers of manholes should be even with the road, to prevent a wheelchair from being thrown off balance.

While curbs are a safety factor to the blind, it is best that they be cut down at ramp sites to provide easy access to and from ramps for the physically handicapped (Gutman and Gutman, 1968).

Inside the School

Entrance

Gutman and Gutman (1968) state that the door *should* be at least 90 mm (3 feet) wide to allow room for the wheelchair to pass. It ought to open inwardly and should not be double-action swing doors. The best doors would be some that are not too heavy, because they would otherwise be too difficult to push open.

Doors that are operated electrically, hydraulically, or pneumatically, may be used also. Those which open from mat contact are the most suitable, since the door will remain open as long as there is pressure on the mat. Revolving doors are not usable by wheelchair patients under any circumstances.

Door handles should be within easy reach to the wheelchair

person. A minimum distance of 42 inches above the floor is suggested, and lever-type knobs are recommended. The knob ought to be readily gripped. Also, it is best that the door have a generous depth of kicking plate.

Thresholds should not exceed one-half inch. If it is necessary to make outside doors draftproof, a piece of plastic tubing that compresses under pressure may be used.

Hallways and Corridors

While carpeted floors may be desirable for the majority of the population, they often cause difficulty in mobility for those students in wheelchairs. Hallways should be wide enough to allow plenty of room for the manipulation of wheelchairs. Handrails ought to be provided along both walls of the halls, and entrances from the hallway to other rooms in the building must be smooth.

To prevent damage to the walls from wheelchairs, the lower portion of the corridor walls may be covered by a wainscot of material. This should be a material that is resistant to impact, scraping, and cutting (Birch and Johnstone, 1975).

Buildings with Two or More Stories

When the school building exceeds more than one story, it is obvious that an elevator will be necessary for the transportation of the physically handicapped person from one level to another. The elevator should be large enough to accommodate a wheelchair and as many passengers as are expected to ride at one time. Control buttons must be placed at a level convenient to the handicapped and the person in wheelchair. A height of 42 inches from the floor is recommended.

Classroom

Physically handicapped children need a larger area in which to maneuver than do normal children. Calovini (1969) writes that 60 square feet of floor space per child should be used as a guide. The space between the desks has to allow adequate room for wheelchairs to pass. Support rails fixed to the walls near the doors and windows are also needed. The ceiling ought to consist of firm fixings at all points, and lockers, cabinets, and work areas have to be arranged where the handicapped child can use them while seated in the wheelchair.

It is necessary that the desks be of such a height that a wheelchair can fit comfortably under them. Some students may prefer to carry a lapboard with them that serves as a writing and study surface. Once in the classroom, the student may exhibit few limitations and may require little additional attention (Rusalem, 1962).

Dining Hall

It is recommended that dining tables be rectangular in shape, with a surface of thirty inches above the floor. There should be nothing around the table to prevent the knees of wheelchair patients from fitting comfortably beneath. The floors *should* be of a nonslip material. The slide for serving trays ought to be at least 34 inches wide and 32 inches from the floor (Gutman and Gutman, 1968).

Some physically handicapped students may need to rest after lunch; therefore, it is necessary that a room with cots be provided for this purpose (Nelliest, 1970).

Gymnasium

The physically handicapped should by all means be included in the physical activities they are capable of participating. These activities include archery, darts, craftmaking, and swimming, etc.

A ramp should be provided for the entrance of the wheelchair patient into the pool, the rails are needed around the edges of the pool.

Gutman and Gutman (1968) state that the entire gymnasium area must be made available to the physically handicapped, in the event they might wish to be spectators at athletic events. It is necessary that there be sufficient room beside the bleachers for the placement of wheelchairs and ramps, and ample doorways ought to be provided for the entrance into the gymnasium.

Auditoriums

In the auditorium there *should* be special seating sections for those in wheelchairs, with access to the stage and dressing rooms. The physically handicapped persons should be able to be participators or observers. Ramps, handrails, and ample doorways provide easy entrance for the physically handicapped here, as in all sections of the building.

Offices

Wide doorways to accommodate wheelchairs would make offices accessible to the handicapped, and offices should have room enough for comfortable manipulation of the wheelchair.

Libraries

A helpful librarian is more than glad to assist anyone in obtaining a book. It would be to the handicapped child's advantage, however, to have card catalogues, etc., at a level s/he can reach without difficulty. Again, tables must be high enough to accommodate the placement of a wheelchair under them.

Bathrooms

It is recommended that toilet facilities join the classroom and the cubicles are wide enough to accommodate wheelchairs. The doors should be wide enough to provide comfortable access to the bathroom. Also, it should be pointed out that standard doors may be replaced by accordian-pleated doors, which take less space.

Handrails should be provided in the individual cubicles to aid the handicapped child in swinging from the wheelchair to the toilet seat. Handrails would preferably be 1.5 inches in diameter, with a clearance of 1.5 inches from the wall. There should be a horizontal rail on each side of the toilet stall. The height of these handrails ought to be approximately 33 inches from the floor.

A wall-hung commode is the most desirable for the handicapped child, and it should be one in which the height may be adjusted to suit the average wheelchair user. Frontal approach and easy floor cleaning in the surrounding areas are some of its advantages. The recommended height from the floor to the toilet seat is 20 inches, and the cubicle *should* measure 36 inches wide and 66 inches deep, with the toilet in the middle rear. The flushing device would be a conveniently positioned lever or a pull knob.

Wash basins should be hung on the wall by brackets or set in a counter top. It is desirable that there be no pedestals or supporting legs to interfere with the knees of the person in a wheelchair, and a 30–inch clearance from the floor to the sink apron ought to be provided. The faucets should be easy to manipulate and all hot pipes insulated to prevent the handicapped child from being burned from contact with the pipes.

Mirrors *should* be no more than 36 inches above the floor and placed near the wash basin if possible (Gutman and Gutman, 1968).

Water Fountains

Water fountains located on each floor are advisable. Gutman and Gutman (1968) say that the controls must be easy to operate by hand and should be located in the front. The fountain ought to be approximately 36 inches above the floor, and it should not be recessed. There should be a paper-cup dispenser within easy reach of wheelchair people next to the fountain.

Switches

Switches located 42 inches from the floor are best, and all control buttons for signals and alarms should also be located at this height. It is suggested that telephones be attached to the wall with the dial 48 inches from the floor, and phones with push-button dialing are preferable (Gutman and Gutman, 1968).

Fire Safety Measures

It must be remembered that the handicapped child is not able to move as rapidly in evacuating a building as others. In a multi-storied building, elevators often cease to operate and may trap occupants between floors. When the handicapped child exits the building, his route must be paved, and all curbs that are part of escape routes should be rolled (Birch and Johnstone, 1975).

Safe Movement in the Building

It may be difficult for the handicapped child to move through the corridors. Most doors open into rooms, but if they do not, it is desirable that they open against a wall to eliminate a door from hitting a child. Open doors should not reduce the width of the corridors.

Automatic door closers must be avoided when dealing with physically handicapped children, because although they close the door, they also make it more difficult to open the door. Also, many handicapped children may lack the strength to open the doors.

If there are rooms in which the child works alone, an emergency call button in each teaching area is recommended. These ought to be placed where they can be reached by a child who has fallen from a chair or wheelchair.

It is recommended that sharp edges and corners be eliminated as much as possible, because the rounded corners on cabinets and other pieces of furniture are less dangerous.

In spaces such as toilet stalls or enclosed carrels where the lock is controlled from the inside, provisions must be made for its access from the outside. This provides for immediate removal of someone who has fallen or fainted.

It is preferable that all the glass in a building for the handicapped be either nonbreakable tempered glass or wire glass. Glass should be avoided at such heights where the handicapped child might fall against it.

An emergency generator is required by most building codes, because this would operate an elevator in case of emergency and prevent children from being trapped within (Birch and Johnstone, 1975).

Conclusion

All fifty United States now require that all new state-owned and –financed buildings be accessible to the handicapped. While private buildings are not affected by laws preventing architectural barriers, many private businesses are becoming aware of the needs of the handicapped. Many hotel chains (Holiday Inns®, Howard

Johnson Corporation, Ramada Inns®, and Travelodge Corporation, among others) have included special rooms for the handicapped. Hertz® and Avis® have rental cars with hand controls available in larger cities (Green, 1973). Many airlines require special training programs in handling the handicapped for their employees.

Increased public knowledge toward architectural barriers will result in fewer barriers. The goal of educators and the public should be total elimination of architectural barriers. When this has been accomplished, handicapped people will be better able to function as first-class citizens.

The following checklist, Structure 1, was developed from information presented in this chapter. It is designed to provide a general check to indicate architectural barriers to the physically handicapped in school buildings.

CHECKLIST

	YES	NO
ENTRANCES		
Ramp		
Handrails		
Door		
3 feet wide		
Opens inwardly		
Opens with slight pressure		
Handles (42 inches above floor)		
Thresholds (maximum 1/2 inch)		
OUTSIDE		
Shallow ramps (1 foot in 12 feet)		
Walks (nonslick)		
Grating bars (right angles to the direction of travel)		
Manhole covers (even with the road)		
Curbs (cut down at ramp sites)		
HALLWAYS AND CORRIDORS		
Wide enough for manipulation of wheelchairs		
Handrails		
MULTISTORIED BUILDINGS		
Elevator		
Large enough to accommodate wheelchair and passengers		
Control buttons (42 inches from floor)		
CLASSROOM		
Adequate space between desks		
Support rails fixed to the walls		
Cabinets (usable while seated in a wheelchair)		
Desks (can a wheelchair fit under it?)		

Structure 1.

DINING HALLS		
Tables		
Rectangular		
30 inches above the floor		
Floors (nonslip materials)		
Serving slide (34 inches wide and 32 inches from the floor)		
GYMNASIUM		
Ramp (into the pool)		
Rails (around the pool)		
Access to bleachers		
AUDITORIUM		
Special seating sections		
Access to stage		
Access to dressing rooms		
OFFICES		
Adequate doorways		
Room for wheelchair manipulation		
LIBRARY		
Card catalogues (reachable level)		
Tables (high enough for wheelchair placement)		
BATHROOMS		
Cubicles (wide enough to accommodate wheelchairs)		
Handrails (in cubicles)		
1 1/2 inches in diameter		
1 1/2 inches from the wall		
33 inches from the floor		
Wash basins		
30 inch clearance from the floor to the sink		
Faucets (easy to manipulate)		

Hot pipes (insulated)		
Mirrors		
36 inches above floor		
Near wash basin		
WATER FOUNTAINS		
Located on each floor		
Controls (hand operated)		
Controls (in front)		
36 inches above the floor		
SWITCHES		
42 inches from the floor		
SAFETY MEASURES		
Exit routes paved		
Escape route curbs rolled		
All doors open into rooms		
Call buttons (in areas the child will be alone)		
Corners on cabinets rounded		
Locked areas accessible from the outside		
Glass		
Nonbreakable tempered glass		
Emergency generator		

REFERENCES

Birch, J.W. and Johnstone, B.K.: *Designing Schools and Schooling for the Handicapped.* Springfield, Thomas, 1975.

Calovini, G.: *The Principal Looks at Classes for the Physically Handicapped.* Washington, D. C., Council on Exceptional Children, 1969.

Green, H.G.: *Removing Barriers from the Pathways of the Handicapped.*

Human Needs. U.S. Dept of Health, Education and Welfare, Rehabilitative Services, 1973.

Gutman, E.M. and Gutman, C.R.: *Wheelchair to Independence.* Springfield, Thomas, 1968.

May, E.E., Waggoner, N.R., and Hotte, E.B.: *Independent Living for the Handicapped and the Elderly.* Boston, Houghton, 1974.

Nelliest, I.: *Planning Buildings for Handicapped Children.* Springfield, Thomas, 1970.

Rusalem, H.: *Guiding the Physically Handicapped College Student.* New York, Bureau of Publications, Columbia U Pr, 1962.

Chapter 7

THE SCHOOL'S RESPONSIBILITY IN VOCATIONAL PLACEMENT OF THE PHYSICALLY HANDICAPPED PERSON

IN DISCUSSING the school's responsibility in vocational placement of the physically handicapped person, the author is primarily concerned with the client or school counselor at a school for the physically handicapped or at a public or private school in the area of work-study.

The author realizes that not all public and private schools have work-study programs for handicapped youngsters, but many do, and certainly, they are desirable programs. Most schools for the physically handicapped person have a placement process for this individual. It is the belief of the author that all schools have a responsibility in placing individuals in a vocational capacity, if these individuals do not intend to go on to college and pursue an area of academics.

The information contained in this chapter is designed to assist the counselor with the often difficult task of placement of the physically handicapped person. It is also intended to stimulate the creativity of the counselor in regard to activities of the placement process and follow-up of the client. Too often, these activities are considered by the school counselor to be routine and elementary. However, the effective counselor must always be cognizant of those placement opportunities that are continually arising and be prepared to utilize them to the fullest. Consistent placement of the physically handicapped will come from hard work and persistence, not from demand for one's client's services.

Placement is considered as an integral service provided by vocational rehabilitation and, as such, is an inseparable part of the habilitation process. It is not to be considered as a menial, subprofessional task relegated to others or left to chance. The challenge of placement should represent a stimulus to develop greater insights and intellectual understanding and to nurture a professional attitude toward placement that will not allow satisfaction with anything less than a superior performance in this aspect of work.

Client Preparation

In determination of the client's readiness for a work situation, there are several considerations to be made at the outset. Many counselors use some type of a job-readiness test. Such a test may be devised by the counselor to fit his own needs or may be a standard form used within his agency. Usually the test will require only *yes* or *no* answers and be easily administered to the client. Keep in mind that some of your clients may not be able to read, write, or speak and the ease of administration is of utmost importance. A simple check list is often the answer to use the readiness test for the physically handicapped client. Items or categories to be considered may include questions about the client's work history and the understanding of its importance, the employment application, preparing for the job interview, conduct while waiting for the interview, conduct during the interview, the termination of the interview session, proper behavior on the job, proper dress for the job, and physical capabilities, etc.

The following is an example of one section of a hypothetical job-readiness test:

While on the job.

1. If we cannot get along with other workers, we may be fired.

   Yes _____   No _____

2. The best way to get the respect of your boss and other workers is to be dependable and have a good attitude.

   Yes _____   No _____

3. Good cooperation is to talk loudly and to complain about the job assigned to you.

   Yes _____   No _____

4. If I am not satisfied with my work, I should just walk out without explaining to anyone.

Yes _____   No _____

5. A person with good manners knows how to talk with people pleasantly.

Yes _____   No _____

In addition to the readiness tests, one may wish to use some type of self-rating scale for the client. Remember that these evaluation instruments may be administered orally to the client, if there is suspicion that he will not grasp the full meaning of the form, questions, etc., or if he is physically unable to write.

Final evaluation of the client's readiness for work will possibly center around five basic questions: (1) Does this client have the physical capacity to engage in productive activity? (2) Does this client have the necessary skills for the type of employment considered? (3) Does this client have the basic intellectual skills to permit him to work in the type situation being considered? (4) What are the client's attitudes toward work, his family, himself? (5) Will those around him, the important people in his life, be able to accept him as a worker?

Another type of readiness test, useful in some instances, follows (Fig. 3).

Normally, the answers to the first three of these questions will have become apparent to the school counselor during the earlier portion of the habilitation process. The answers to the other questions are not easily quantifiable and, therefore, may best be answered by the physically handicapped person himself, via a questionnaire or test of the type mentioned previously. The total results of such inventories can be of great help to the school counselor in helping clients to reach a more satisfactory level of job readiness.

The sources of the client's vocational interests is of a special concern in working with the physically handicapped client. It must be determined whether interests are based on actual work experience, readings, observations, influence of family or friends,

Name _____ Date _____

Question or Statement	Response	Points
1. May I help you? (states purpose)	_____	_____
2. What is your name?	_____	_____
3. How old are you?	_____	_____
4. What is your birthdate?	_____	_____
5. Have you worked before?	_____	_____
6. What kind of work can you do?	_____	_____
7. What is your Social Security number? (give credit if card is presented)	_____	_____
8. Are you single or married?	_____	_____
9. What is your address?	_____	_____
10. Give me a phone number where you can be reached.	_____	_____
11. What are your parents' names?	_____	_____
12. How do you like school?	_____	_____
13. What do you do with your leisure time or for fun?	_____	_____
14. How much do you weigh?	_____	_____
15. How tall are you?	_____	_____
16. and 17. Give me the names of two persons as references.	_____	_____
18. How would you get to work?	_____	_____
19. What are your physical defects?	_____	_____
20. (Give a point for good posture, sitting and standing.)		_____
21. (Give a point for good manners, such as saying, "Thank you.")		_____
22. (Give a point for good diction.)		_____

TOTAL POINTS _____

Self-Rating Scale

Things I try to do:	Always	Sometimes	Never
Be on time			
Do my work			
Get along			
Never talk back			
Do my best			

Figure 3.

or other miscellaneous factors. Another important consideration will be the length of time that the vocational interest has been expressed. Many times, the physically handicapped person will change interests almost daily depending upon what mood he is in, what he has seen on television the night before, etc. The school counselor must be on guard against an almost constant change in the goals of this client.

The *marginal* worker is often a thorn in the school counselor's side, especially in dealing with the physically handicapped. Upon close examination, it is often determined that these workers are marginal because they have never been taught the basic skills necessary to compare vocationally. Statistical data reveal that only 10 percent to 15 percent of the labor force lose their jobs because of lack of actual ability to do the job. In the special category of the physically handicapped, this percentage is somewhat lower. What then are the major reasons for loss of employment? In order of frequency they are: lack of initiative, carelessness, uncooperative attitude, laziness, tardiness, and lack of ability. It is important to note that these are basically traits that could be corrected with the proper guidance of the client.

When the handicapped worker presents a placement problem for the counselor, s/he may want to consider various procedures for remediation of those deficit areas. Individual or group-counseling sessions may be held to help the client to realize the attributes and information needed to locate, obtain and retain employment. These sessions may include discussion of why work is important (not only from the economic standpoint but for other reasons as well), what media to utilize in learning of job prospects, how to fill out applications, where to go for assistance in obtaining employment, proper dress codes, employee responsibility to the employer, etc. Information gained from such counseling assists the client in enjoying job stability.

Although it is an important consideration, the procedure that the counselor uses to impart this basic knowledge to the marginal worker is not as important as the objectives. Counselors have used various techniques to accomplish this, including the use of former clients who have been successfully placed, interested employers, and/or printed material and visual aids. The thing to remember seems to be the determination of what the individual needs to know about his job behavior in order to preclude some of the problems.

It is extremely important to the physically handicapped person that he understand that it is not necessarily bad to be turned down for a job. The school counselor should take adequate steps to assure the client that almost everyone that enters the labor market is, at one time or another, denied employment. Increased employer contacts made as soon as possible after the initial denial of employment will help the client to overcome some of the anxiety and depression that he may be feeling at this point.

The school counselor may occasionally find that a client was turned down because of a company policy that prohibits the hiring of an individual until he has returned a second or third time to ask for the job. This policy, although not too common, is designed to discourage applicants that have only a cursory interest in the position that is available. Other companies may have some policy against hiring individuals with certain handicapping conditions. These employers should be identified as rapidly as possible and eliminated from the list of possibilities for those clients that do not qualify for employment. This aids the counselor and the client in regard to time, effort, and the preservation of the client's self-concept.

If a client reports an unsuccessful interview, a call to the employer will often reveal the reason for the failure. If it was because of personality factors, more preparations may be necessary before another attempt is made. If it was because of lack of skills, one may want to consider some type of vocational training for the client or perhaps a closer look at the type of employment the client is seeking. In these ways, the employer may help the counselor to help the client become more employable.

In some cases, the client may have to accept employment at a level below his ability level. In these instances, the employer is usually anxious for the client to perform well, so that he can give the client the promotions that are warranted. Under such circumstances, the client should be fully aware of these arrangements by the employer. The counselor must have the whole-hearted commitment of the client before placing the client in such a work setting. If the physically handicapped individual does not understand the possibilities of the employment, he may react with some type of undesirable attitude or behavior. Follow-up of such placement is often needed on an extended basis to make certain that the client is being given due consideration for advancement in his job.

Counselor—Employer Relations

The counselor must always maintain a positive attitude in approaching the employer, because his/her reaction is mirrored to the client. One should be enthusiastic and nonapologetic, but certain that one has something to sell to the employer.

The counselor cannot place someone that he himself cannot accept, s/he does not know, or someone in whom he places little confidence. This would indicate, again, the need for a comprehensive evaluation of the client.

In order to establish good rapport, one must level with the employer. Do not, under any circumstances, misrepresent the client or his abilities. If the counselor is to maintain good relations in the job community, he must be honest with each client referred for an interview. If in doubt about the client's ability in the job, one may want to suggest a job tryout to determine if the client is suited for employment.

It is well to remember that in all client-employer interviews there is no interference in the communication between the client and the employer. It is very difficult to maintain silence in some instances. However, interference might well diminish the client's chances for employment if it points out his inability to act independently.

It is important in employer relationships that you stress your availability for assistance after placement has been accomplished. Let the employer know that you are not through with the case until both the client and the employer are satisfied with the arrangement. Then make sure that you keep your end of the agreement. The attitude of the counselor is tremendously important. Counselors should be objective in their approach and need not feel that the employer is looking for reasons to reject the client. The "hard-sell" approach may often result in an ineffective attempt at placement in which both the employer and employee may be dissatisfied.

Employers are interested in a client primarily in relation to his/ her marketable skills and job behavior. In contacts with prospective employers, be sure that information regarding the client's skills and behaviors is available. In working with the physically handicapped, many counselors have found it useful to use a *can do* list to assist them in placement attempts. Such a list includes the parts of an operation or the functions of a particular job that a particular client can do well. Such an approach is effective because it focuses attention on ability of the client rather than disability. Remember, the client has a service, talents and/or skills to sell. He is not merely asking for a job.

Most employers are perceptive enough to sense a client's inability to accept his disability. Job readiness always includes being prepared to cope with the work environment, as well as having the necessary skills for the job. Reaction to disability is an area that may require intensive work with the client, the employer, other employees, and the general public. Counselors are urged not to appeal to the employer to hire the handicapped client because of his charitable or humanitarian interests or even because of his concern as a taxpayer with the problems of the handicapped. By approaching the employer in a businesslike fashion, explaining the merits of the client and how he can be of benefit to the employer, the counselor will enjoy a better reception and a more lasting relationship with prospective employers.

Talking with employers need not only be for the purpose of placing a client. Most employers will appreciate knowing about vocational rehabilitation and how the school can be of service to them. By explaining that services would be available to his employees should they or any member of their family ever need it, the counselor should be able to help the employer realize that the counselor's service should be listed as an asset for his company.

Even if the counselor is never able to help one of the employees of a firm or place a client in the establishment, he will have helped the school and the disabled individuals in the community by explaining the work that is being done. One may find that some of the employers that were talked with later have heard of the school through these contacts of public information. Before approaching the employer to hire a client, learn as much about his company as possible. This initial investment of time will alert the counselor to many things (company policy, specifics of the services rendered, or the products manufactured by the concern, etc.). This information, when used wisely, can be used to tip the balance in favor of a good placement for the client.

When visiting a place of business to talk with an employer concerning placement, know what clients are ready to work, so that you can talk with the employer in definite terms. It helps no one when a job is offered and there is no client ready to fill the opening. Whatever the occasion permits, the counselor may wish to use a portfolio of work samples to show the employer what a particular client can do or produce. In some instances, this can be a very persuasive tool for the counselor.

Usually, the counselor meets the challenge of the employer interview alone. In some instances, however, s/he may wish to team with another counselor, a representative of the state employment service, and/or the client. It has been found that a team approach to the employer has produced excellent results in most cases. Two counselors seem to answer questions and objections more easily and quickly than does one. If the employment service representative knows the employer and has a good relationship established with the concern, the wise counselor will utilize this person to the fullest. In addition to making a good initial impression on the employer, he may be able to provide much information about the employer's biases, interests, attitudes, etc.

The use of professional jargon and rehabilitation terminology when talking with an employer may have an adverse effect on placement opportunities. While its use may make the counselor feel more comfortable, it is usually not acceptable to the employer.

To sell oneself, one's client, and one's program more effectively, the counselor needs to be aware of the problems with which the employer must deal when employing a handicapped person. Some of the most commonly encountered objections to employment of the physically handicapped are:

1. Legal considerations and Workmen's Compensation Laws
2. Architectural barrier or physical plant limitations
3. General job requirements
4. Training and education levels of supervisors and fellow employees
5. Safety requirements of the job
6. Reactions of the public and/or other employees to the client

There are numerous methods useful in dealing with the above-listed problems, but the counselor must first understand them thoroughly. Know the policy of insurance companies and Workmen's Compensation toward employment of the physically handicapped client. Try to work around most of the problems associated with architectural barriers, and education of fellow employees and supervisors before approaching an employer. Be fully aware of the general job requirements beforehand, and be certain that the client is able to perform adequately. Know the facts and figures of the safety record of the physically handicapped. Keep in mind, however, that the employer does not want to be bombarded with statistics, except as they relate to specific questions. Counselors that approach an employer "armed to the teeth" with statistical data may be extremely irritating to an employer. Wait until specific questions about the work record of the client are asked before volunteering information.

Employer Receptivity

Attitudes of employers toward the hiring of physically handicapped individuals are obviously crucial to the vocational success of physically handicapped people.

A counselor faced with the problem of placement must be well equipped to show the benefits and advantages of hiring the handicapped client. The counselor must be convinced that s/he has a *marketable* item and need not provide ready-made excuses for that item. Within the last few years, an ever-increasing amount of information has become available to placement personnel concerning the work histories and general vocational capabilities of the physically handicapped. The effective counselor must keep abreast of this information flow in order to properly represent every client charged to him.

The President's Committee on Employment of the Handicapped (1963) stated that job areas for the physically handicapped client fell into the following categories: service, 30 percent; unskilled, 21.2 percent; semiskilled, 19.3 percent; clerical, 12.0 percent; family worker, 6.2 percent; agriculture, 55.9 percent; and skilled, 5.4 percent. This information simply reiterates the fact that the physically handicapped client can perform a variety of tasks successfully.

The counselor should emphasize the fact that the placement of the client in his business, in most cases, increases efficiency. Numerous examples of good work records, low absenteeism, and increased production, etc. are available as an added tool for use by the counselor. Too often, personnel in charge of placement are prone to take the attitude that the employer is doing them a favor in taking on the physically handicapped as an employee.

Although many negative conditions and policies still existent in the community prohibit or diminish the opportunities of the physically handicapped for appropriate work and living conditions, national movements to modify and hopefully eliminate these conditions are under way in increasing numbers. Parents have organized themselves, nationally and locally, and have initiated action to remove the blocks and to lessen the gap. Gradually, more services are being provided by municipalities and by private and community organizations that assist counselors in overcoming some of the traditional barriers in dealing with prospective employers.

Questionable Assumptions as to Placement

Many of the placement assumptions concerning the physically handicapped client, have, over the years, persisted, in spite of efforts to dispel them. These assumptions have been handed down, somewhat uncritically, to succeeding generations of counselors and have interfered with effective and proper placement for many physically handicapped clients.

The first assumption is that the level of intelligence necessary for a particular job is always known. By making such an assumption, the possibilities for placement are severely limited. This basic assumption has been by the fact that counselors persist in acting within this narrow framework. Rehabilitation counselors and rehabilitation workers in general have developed stereotypes for certain limiting conditions. A good example of this is the still-common practice of training paraplegics in small appliance repair, watch repair, etc. Quite obviously, many paraplegics have mental capabilities far exceeding those required to assemble a steam iron or coffee pot. The same situation exists in the area of other physical handicapping conditions. Traditionally, counselors have placed these individuals in menial, unskilled work situations, despite the fact that many of these clients could qualify for and succeed in other types of employment.

It is unlikely that this first assumption of a known level of intelligence for a certain job can be overcome to any large extent until counselors and other rehabilitation personnel understand the multifaceted environment of the job environment. Factors of supervision, physical surroundings, general morale, and job readiness all play an important part in influencing the retarded worker's intelligence in his particular vocational tasks.

A second assumption is that the retarded individual is satisfied with employment in certain occupational fields. Because physically handicapped individuals often have not been exposed to realistic vocational goals, this type of client will sometimes indicate a choice of vocations that is both beyond his capability and his understanding. The counselor must constantly be on guard to assure the proper placement of this client in a situation that will be conducive to success. A statement often heard in relation to the physically handicapped is that they have an increased tolerance to boredom. It seems unrealistic that great pains are taken to assure that the normal worker is not bored by his tasks; this is often overlooked in placement of the physically handicapped client. Whether the counselor can obtain interesting vocational placements for all of the clients in his caseload is debatable. However, care should be taken to make placements on the basis of suitability, rather than on dangerous generalizations.

The implications of the above assumptions are many and varied. If more objectivity could be built into placement efforts, the segregation of the physically handicapped worker from the general labor force could be minimized. Because these clients are labeled as somewhat inferior, counselors have forced themselves to function within rather narrow confines. It has been proved over and over again that expectations have a tremendous impact on performance of employees. If counselors expect more from clients, cannot success in areas heretofore deemed out of reach be anticipated?

There is no denying that differences exist in intelligence levels and that differences exist in vocational capabilities. It is imperative, however, that methods of evaluating these differences be reexamined in the hope that some of the traditional *idea-killing* assumptions can be erased as handicaps in effective placement of the physically handicapped.

Proposals for Action

For the physically handicapped person, employment is a burst of sunlight—particularly for those who never worked before and those who had never dared hope of work.

The following are suggestions for continuing programs that will eventually result in employment opportunities for almost all of the physically handicapped individuals capable of productive employment.

The federal government should encourage training projects in occupations not usually considered within the capabilities of the physically handicapped, in order to demonstrate their wide range of employability.

Employers should be encouraged to review and scale down their educational requirements for jobs. Some employers still require high-school diplomas for relatively unskilled work. This is an unrealistic prerequisite.

Encouragement should be given to job redesign—removing routine functions from existing jobs, grouping functions together, and creating new, lesser-skilled jobs the physically handicapped can perform. Job redesign is possible for both white- and blue-collar jobs. It serves to make better use of highly skilled persons by not wasting their time on routine functions. It can open new job opportunities for the physically handicapped.

Physically handicapped workers should be paid no less than prevailing wages in the area. Physically handicapped individuals are entitled to the same wage scale as the nonhandicapped, provided they can perform on the job satisfactorily.

More inplant on-the-job training programs for the physically handicapped should be encouraged. Here, industry provides training on the premises. More industry-wide training and employment projects should be encouraged also.

Hopefully, with the inception of such projects as outlined above, school counselors will see many of the barriers to effective placement fall by the wayside. The physically handicapped deserve a chance to prove themselves in competitive situations, and it is up to the counselor to provide those opportunities.

In this chapter, the author has assumed that the reader knows that the school has a responsibility in vocational placement not only of physically handicapped students, but of all students who choose not to pursue a college program. The major emphasis has been on the vocational counselor placing the student or client. The author fully realizes that all schools do not have vocational programs, but certainly all educators would agree that all schools should have vocational programs. The physically handicapped student is unique because of his physical characteristics. This makes many potential employers skeptical of the physically handicapped person's ability to do a particular job. Research, though, indicates that physically handicapped people work harder, are more appreciative of having a job, are not tardy very often, and are absent from work far less than the so-called normal person.

The regular or private school has a responsibility for helping physically handicapped people choose a vocational course if they are not going to college, and certainly the special school for physically handicapped people would have a similar obligation. When a youngster leaves high school s/he should be prepared to either go to college or to work. This applies to all youngsters, whether normal physically handicapped, or mentally retarded, etc. If this philosophy is followed in the schools throughout the United States, the vocational counselor will play a very important role, and the schools' responsibility to the physically handicapped person will be met.

REFERENCE

The President's Committee on Employment of the Handicapped: Guide to Job Placement of the Mentally Retarded. Washington, D.C., U.S. Govt Print. Office, 1963.

Chapter 8

SHORT-TERM EDUCATIONAL GOALS FOR CHILDREN WITH SERIOUS HEALTH PROBLEMS

SINCE the advent of mainstreaming, it is necessary that teachers become aware of the many problems they might encounter in children with serious health problems. This chapter deals with several diseases found in school-age children, how to recognize them, and how to best educate those who have them. The diseases to be discussed are cystic fibrosis, Friedreich's ataxia, heart disease, muscular dystrophy, and some forms of leukemia.

Cystic Fibrosis

Cystic fibrosis is the most common cause of death from genetic disorder in the United States. One in fifteen hundred children are born in this country with cystic fibrosis, and one in twenty-five Caucasians carry the gene, making it the most common cause of chronic lung disease in Caucasian children (Shwachman, 1972). Cystic fibrosis is found less frequently in the Negroid race and is almost unheard of in Orientals.

The name *cystic fibrosis* was coined by a pathologist, Dorothy Anderson. Anderson found, in children dead from this then-supposed lung disease, that there was also an involvement of the pancreas. This disorder of the pancreas prevented absorption of vitamin A. It was also marked by numerous cysts and fibrous scarring, thus the name *cystic fibrosis*.

Symptoms

Cystic fibrosis may be detected in some cases at birth. This is marked by irregularities of the intestinal tract, causing blockage. If found soon enough, the blockage may be removed surgically.

In older children, many other symptoms may be noted. The

child may have frequent stools that are bulky and greasy, with an extremely unpleasant odor, the result of the undigested fats due to the malfunctioning pancreas. The child may also have an unusual appetite or not gain an adequate amount of weight because of the high loss of calories. Frequent and long-lasting lung infections, very often resulting in a secondary infection, are often found in the child with cystic fibrosis. Persistent coughs and wheezing, commonly incorrectly diagnosed as asthma, may also be a sign. He may also lose a large amount of salt in his perspiration during the summer, which must be replaced intravenously. This last symptom also provides a means of diagnosis by determining the concentration of salt in the perspiration.

A child with severe cystic fibrosis may often have a very distorted appearance. His chest is rounded due to the size of his hyperinflated lungs. Because he has larger amounts of stools and more gas, his stomach is often distended. On occasion, his fingers may have a bulbous rounding on the fingertips. Survival of these children rarely goes beyond adolescence (May, 1954).

Important Factors

There are six important factors that a teacher of a child with cystic fibrosis should keep in mind. First, his cough is *not* contagious. The child may be embarrassed and try to hide this cough, but this should be avoided because collection of the mucus in the lungs could become dangerous and should be expelled. Therefore, the teacher should see that little attention is paid to his cough, and that the other students accept it, so that he will feel at ease to cough when necessary.

The child with cystic fibrosis may also have an abnormal appetite and take second or third helpings during the meals. This should be allowed and little attention should be attributed to this fact. If the child is on a diet, it should be followed as closely as is feasible, unless, however, it is extremely different from that of his peers. It is better to have an occasional variation from his diet so that he will not feel different from his friends. Because of his large appetite, he should also be excused from class for the restroom whenever necessary. He also may take a synthetic pancreatic enzyme for digestion.

This child may not have as much stamina as his classmates, but he should be encouraged to participate as much as he physically can. However, he must not be allowed to overexert himself in order to hide his illness. Unless he is receiving additional salt, he should be watched in hot weather to see that he does not perspire too much.

There is no reason why the cystic fibrotic children should not be as bright as their peers, and sometimes they appear more so because they tend to devote their time more to their studies than to physical activities. Naturally, they should not be held back intellectually because of their illness.

The final and most important thing for the teacher to remember is this: Treat the child as much like the other children as possible. The child is quite aware of his difference and that he may be a burden to his family, both financially and emotionally. His exact treatment, though, is determined by the psychological and physical adjustment of the individual child (Bleck and Nagel, 1975).

Friedreich's Ataxia

Friedreich's ataxia is another disease a teacher may encounter in the classroom. It is "an inherited (familial) disease in which there is progressive degeneration of the sensory cells in the dorsal ganglia and nerves to the limbs and trunk (peripheral nerves)" (Merritt, 1970).

Symptoms

Friedreich's ataxia (FA) usually becomes evident in the first or second decade of life, but in rare cases, it may be detected in early infancy. Because of the weakened conditions of the limbs and trunk, the child with Friedreich's ataxia may fall frequently and walk with a lurching gait. The impairment of fine motor control is evidenced by lack of agility, clumsiness, and a shaky erratic handwriting. The speech of the child often becomes slurred, and in the infant, feeding may eventually become impossible because of the effects of the disease on the upper extremities. As the disease progresses, the child may evidence diminished or even absent deep tendon reflexes with an increasing loss of sense of vibration and position in space. Atrophy of the limbs may also result.

Bleck and Nagel (1975) state that skeletal deformities, such as club foot, high arches, and hammer toe, may accompany Friedreich's ataxia and that 80 percent of teens and young adults having the disease also suffer from curvature of the spine.

Heart abnormalities may occur at any time during the life of the FA victim. In a study reported by Bleck and Nagel (1975), EKGs were found to undergo a significant change in over 90 percent of known patients. Constriction of both the aorta from the heart and the main artery to the lungs may occur, accompanied by irregular heart beats, murmurs, or an enlargement of the heart itself.

In many reported cases, the FA patient suffers from eye problems such as optic nerve atrophy and retinal degeneration, which occur later in the course of the disease. Another condition called *nystagmus,* a rapid oscillation of the eyeball, is often observed. The child may have difficulty with visual tracking and have no normal saccadic eye movements. Because they may even have an actual loss of visual acuity, these children may not want to read, or might even lack the ability to do so.

Progression of Disease

For many children with Friedreich's ataxia, there may be a gradual deterioration of mental ability. Seizures occur much more frequently in these children than in other children. Their bodies have little control of the blood sugar, and abnormal amounts of insulin may be produced. Other spinocerebellar degeneration may also take place.

The progression of Friedreich's ataxia may be either rapid or slow. In people who inherit the disease recessively, death was found to occur on the average at age twenty-six and one-half years. On the other hand, those with dominant inheritance lived, on the average, thirty-nine and one-half years (Bleck and Nagel, 1975).

In therapy for Friedreich's ataxia, antiseizure and heart drugs may be used when needed. Medication may be used to relieve tremors, but this frequently does not help. The most important therapy, both physically and emotionally, is the best possible correction of any physical deformities which may be found.

Educational Implications

It is important that children who have Friedreich's ataxia be kept in a regular classroom for as long as possible. The teacher should remember that they need a great deal of encouragement and motivation due to the fact that their physical impairments may cause them to lag behind their peers in many activities.

If the child reaches the point where he can no longer remain in a regular classroom, a suitable school for the handicapped should be recommended. The teacher should be familiar with the special aids and physical therapy implements which may be necessary. If the child has difficulty in writing, s/he should be provided with special tools for grasping pencils or perhaps even the use of an electric typewriter. Above all, the teacher needs to encourage the child to do as well as s/he possibly can.

If, as in some cases, the disease has slow progress, the child may be able to finish the regular high school. Following this, s/he may be sent to a vocational training school with emphasis placed on those skills that do not require fine motor coordination, or s/he may choose to go to a college or university. Those who do not reach this stage may live a useful life and learn to function adequately in today's society.

Heart Defect

With the numerous lifesaving techniques available today, it is not uncommon to have a child in the class who suffers from a heart defect. There are two general types of defects: *congenital,* indicating that the child was born with the defect, and *acquired,* the disease occurs some time after birth.

Congenital heart defects occur twenty times more often in children than do acquired defects (the opposite is true for adults). In the United States, 6 children of every 1000 born have congenital heart defects. This high incidence would be even higher if stillbirths were included in this figure. However, if the defects are left untreated, by the age of ten years the incidence drops to

1 or 2 per 1000, because some openings close by themselves. Early death usually results from the more serious defects and most frequently occurs within the first few months of life.

To help prevent premature deaths in children, early detection is imperative. Parents and teachers should watch for shortness of breath, fatigue, poor growth and development, chest pains, blueness of lips and nail beds (cyanosis), fainting, and chest deformity. These are all symptoms common to both congenital and acquired defects. If it is suspected that a child has a heart problem, arrangements for an immediate examination by a physician should be made.

Seven types of congenital heart defects frequently found in children are discussed. There are numerous others, but these are the ones most commonly detected.

Patent Ductus Arteriosus

In the unborn fetus, the *ductus arteriosus* may be open, or patent, in order for the blood to bypass the lungs. However, in some cases, it remains patent after birth. This causes the heart to work harder, because the blood passing through the aorta is shunted back to the lungs through the ductus arteriosus. If the opening is wide, which allows a large blood flow, heart failure could result. Digitalis is often helpful in alleviating symptoms, but surgical correction is usually required.

Ventricular Septal Defect

When an opening in the septum which separates the left and right ventricles occurs, it is referred to as a *ventricular septal defect*. Enlargement of the heart results, because of pressure due to the extra work that must be done by the ventricles. The children having this condition are extremely susceptible to lung infections, which may cause an added burden on the heart, causing, in many instances, heart failure. A secondary growth failure often is accompanied with this defect. This defect is also correctable by surgery.

Atrial Septal Defect

Atrial septal defect refers to holes in the septum separating the two atria. If this defect is left untreated, cardiovascular disease may occur in the third decade of life, and heart failure may result in the fourth and fifth decades.

Tetralogy of Fallot

Children with *tetralogy of Fallot,* which is the most common defect found in children a year old or over, constitute three fourths of the cyanosis patients. There are four components of this ailment: a large ventricle septal defect, a right ventricular obstruction, a right ventricular hypertrophy, and an overriding of the ventricular septal defect by the aorta. These children are often referred to as *blue babies* because of the bluish appearance of the lips and nails. The blue coloration is caused by the mixing of poorly oxygenated blood with that blood returned fresh from the lungs. Children with tetralogy of Fallot often suffer from hypoxic spells, characterized by hyperventilation, increasing cyanosis, and fainting.

Transposition of the Great Vessels

In children who have a *transposition of the great vessels,* there is a reversal of the aorta and the pulmonary artery. The pulmonary artery originates from the left instead of the right ventricle and the aorta is with the right instead of left ventricle. This means that poorly oxygenated blood is pumped back through the body and fresh blood is returned to the lungs. If not surgically corrected, 90 percent of these infants die within the first year of life, because of insufficient oxygen and heart failure.

Aortic Stenosis

The heart defect known as *aortic stenosis* is caused by an obstruction in the region of the aortic valve. There are three types: valvular (deformity of the valve itself), supravalvular (narrowing just above the valve), and subvalvular (narrowing just below the valve). The obstruction may cause chest pain because of extreme exertion of the ventricle, and heart failure may eventually result. Children who have aortic stenosis are highly susceptible to bacterial endocarditis and should be closely observed.

Coarctation of the Aorta

Coarctation of the aorta, constriction of the aorta in the region where the large arterial branches to the left arm arise, causes interference with the delivery of blood to the branches of the aorta and beyond. This is characterized by a diminished pulse in the legs and high blood pressure in the arms. Again, as with other defects, heart failure may eventually take place.

Valvular Pulmonic Stenosis

Valvular pulmonic stenosis is caused by a narrowing of the pulmonary valve, accompanied by a muscular obstruction just below the valve. This produces high blood pressure with an added danger of susceptibility to bacterial endocarditis.

Rheumatic Fever and Hypertension

There are two common causes of acquired heart disease, or that which is developed later in the postnatal period. The first of these is *rheumatic fever,* which sometimes follows streptococcal infection (Hughes, 1967). The child may have fever, rashes, subcutaneous nodules, chorea, and carditis. The heart may be left permanently damaged in the area of the mitral and aortic valves. There is always the danger of bacterial endocarditis and recurrence of the fever itself. Due to the extreme weakening of the heart, these children have an extremely limited physical capacity. *Hypertension,* or high blood pressure, the second acquired heart disease, is not as common in children as is rheumatic fever. When it occurs in children, it is often a result of a kidney or endocrine disease and is readily controlled by medication.

Education

It is difficult to give specific and detailed instructions for the education of all children with heart problems, due to the wide variety of diseases and the severity of them in each individual child. However, some generalizations may be made. More often than not, the child should not engage in competitive athletics. If he does, he should have the permission of a physician. He should be encouraged to participate in nonathletic, extracurricular activities, and arrangements for nonphysical job training should be made. The child must be prepared for the social and economic needs of his own future.

The teacher of a child with a heart condition should be familiar with the medications, if any, that the child is taking. She should also be aware of both the child's limitations and potentialities. Many of these children have normal intelligence or above and are adjusted educationally and socially, and should be encouraged to live as full a life as possible.

Muscular Dystrophy

Muscular dystrophy (MD) is defined as "profuse weakness of all muscle groups characterized by a degeneration of muscle cells and their replacement by fat and fibrous tissue." Medical personnel say there are five major types of muscular dystrophy: Duchenne type, progressive, pseudohypertrophic, limb-girdle, and facioscapulohumeral. However, since the Duchenne type is the form most commonly found in school-age children, it will be the only one discussed.

Symptoms

As stated in Chapter 2, there are many symptoms characterizing muscular dystrophy. At approximately three years of age, the child may appear awkward and clumsy, may tend to run on his tiptoes and "walk" up his lower limbs with his hands when rising from a sitting position. He will often have a protruding abdomen and swayback, along with several other skeletal deformities. His appearance may be that of an obese child because of the replacement of the muscles with fatty tissue. Many children with muscular dystrophy are found to be subnormal mentally; 70 percent of these children have IQs in the eighties. The Duchenne type of muscular dystrophy is thought to be sex-linked, occurs more frequently in males, and may be transmitted by the female to the male.

Progression of MD

As the disease progresses, adaptive equipment often becomes necessary. The child should be provided with loose-fitting clothing to insure comfort and wheelchairs, autovans, and lifts for better mobility.

Since the prognosis for muscular dystrophy is bleak, many children and parents become discouraged. It is important to keep the child in good spirits which will help him, his parents, and his peers. The child's life should be made as enjoyable as possible, and at all costs, he must not be led to believe that he is a burden to his family and his friends.

Educational Implications

The teacher of an MD child must remember that he is easily fatigued and may need frequent periods of rest. The teacher also needs to realize this child's physical limitations and be careful not to pressure the child or let him overwork himself. The teacher may use psychometric testing for diagnosis and remediation, and it must be remembered that there is a possibility of mental retardation. Since the disease is progressive, numerous adjustments will have to be made for the child while it runs its course. Above all, the child should be kept as comfortable and as happy as possible.

Overall, the outlook for children with serious diseases is not good. The most important thing for a teacher of children with serious health problems to do is to *encourage*. Encourage the child in everything he does. Urge him to do all that he can, and show him that *his* life is important, too.

Leukemia

Leukemia is a malignancy of the bone marrow in which there is a massive overproduction or abnormal formation of the white blood cells. Usually it is fatal in children, although modern methods of treatment have greatly increased children's survival time. Although the cause of leukemia is not known, it has been found to be related to mongolism, massive amounts of irradiation, and viruses found in animals but not in humans.

Symptoms

A child developing leukemia may show symptoms such as pallor, fatigue, fever, weight loss, pain in the joints, and excessive bruising. It must be pointed out, however, that these symptoms are not specific for leukemia and often occur in other, less serious illnesses. The correct diagnosis must be made by a physician after case study and examination of several blood tests, including studies of the bone marrow where the blood cells are formed.

Educational Implications

More and more children with leukemia are being found in the schools, because the survival rate now for some types has increased beyond six years. The teachers and schools must be prepared to have these students and to take care of their unique needs. Medicines are frequently given, and these potent drugs may produce side effects that may affect the child in school. Children with leukemia often have a tendency toward infection and bleeding, and their physicians should decide when it is safe for the child in school.

REFERENCES

Bleck, E. and Nagel, D.A.: *Physically Handicapped Children.* New York, Grune, 1975.

Hughes, J.C.: *Synopsis of Pediatrics,* 2nd ed. St. Louis, Mosby, 1967.

May, C.D.: *Cystic Fibrosis of the Pancreas in Infants and Children.* Springfield, Thomas, 1954.

Merritt, H.H.: *A Textbook of Neurology.* Philadelphia, Lea & Febiger, 1970.

Schwachman, H.: *Diseases of the Respiratory Tract in Children,* 2nd ed. Philadelphia, Saunders, 1972.

Chapter 9

HOW PARENTAL ATTITUDES AFFECT SCHOOL ADJUSTMENT AND ACHIEVEMENT

IN THE United States, approximately 13 percent of children in the schools are exceptional. All of these children have one thing in common: a biological mother and father. Their lives are molded by the interaction of their exceptionality and family life. Most of these children live with and form personality patterns because of their families, but the environment of each plays a major role in the establishment of personality, whether the child lives with his parents or in a foster home.

Probably at no time or phase in the history of the United States has so much been expected of the small family group. In primitive society, responsibility for child rearing was shared by large family groups: grandparents, aunts, uncles, cousins, as well as of the child's own parents. This is not true in the United States today, although it was true in the rural areas of America fifty years ago. Today, the major burden falls on the young mother, and the phrase used "As the mother is, so is the family." Americans move about for better jobs or more favorable climates; therefore, many young families live many miles away from their relatives. There is often no one close to whom they may turn for guidance in the task of child rearing.

Most exceptional children, excluding the gifted, of course, have a major problem to overcome in building a self-concept that contributes to good adjustment.

The more visible the handicap, the greater the problem of building an acceptable self-concept, and the greater the problem of adjustment, according to most research. Even the high intellect of the gifted child affects his personality and his personal adjustment. Therefore, the old adage "We are the product of our environment" is very true. And, the differentness of the individual accentuates his place in society and has a great influence on personal adjustment.

The remainder of this chapter deals with the most important segment of a person's life: his family and particularly his parents. All the exceptionalities covered not only include the handicap or exceptionality, but also parental adjustment to and acceptance of the condition.

PARENTAL ATTITUDES TOWARD THE PHYSICALLY HANDICAPPED CHILD

Professional concern with being able to understand the global entity of the physically handicapped individual and his capacity to function in the family and society has led to the study of parental attitudes and the dictatorial role they play in the life of the handicapped child. Parental reactions toward the physically handicapped child cover such an extensive range and variance of patterns that the task of encompassing all pertinent data within one chapter is very improbable. Consequently, the general purpose of the present chapter is to explain and enlarge upon certain reaction patterns that are seemingly common enough to warrant description. Initial reaction, lasting and developmental attitudes, the prospectus of attitude change effected through parent counseling; all these are areas of major significance and are dealt with accordingly.

Initial Reaction

In trying to construct a homogenous group of concepts from past research, it was found that agreement could be reached on one general conclusion concerning initial reaction to the birth of a defective child, that concept being, parents, upon hearing of their child's handicap for the first time, react differently in intensity of, rather than kinds of, emotion. Telford and Sawrey (1967) state that "None of these reactions is peculiar to parents of defective children; they are the common reactions of normal people to frustration and conflict." Thurston (1960), in talking with parents of handicapped children, concurs with this idea and reports that "As would be expected, virtually all parents experienced emotional upset and anxiety when they learned they had a handicapped child. While they differed in their initial reaction, most displayed helplessness, grief or guilt in varying degrees."

There seems to be some correlation between the number and kind of handicaps that the child has and the intensity of the parental reaction. This is evident in Baum's (1962) statement that the reactions by parents who had been informed of the birth of a blind or orthopedically imperfect child differed more in degree than in kind from reactions of parents of more globally handicapped children.

Throughout the search for data pertaining to initial parent reaction, nine emotional patterns appeared in print more frequently than others: (1) anxiety, (2) grief, (3) disbelief, (4) emotional upset, (5) shock, (6) helplessness, (7) anger, (8) disappointment, and (9) nonspecific. From this last category, anxiety, guilt, and emotional upset appeared most often.

Thurston (1963), in a study to determine parental attitudes toward cerebral-palsied children, attempted, by use of a psychological device called the *Thurston Sentence Completion Form,* to gain information on a systematic basis. By use of this method, Thurston was able to secure a variety of parental reactions to the initial announcement that their child was physically handicapped. These reactions ranged from shock to rationality. The majority of the parents stated that they were severely disturbed, with the most characteristic emotions being grief, helplessness, and disbelief. Of the parents, 41 percent cried, did not know what to do, or did not believe it. Another 10 percent responded with worry and dread when hearing about their child; 15 percent sought medical assistance upon learning of the child's condition; and an additional 4 percent stated that they were nonspecific as to what they did. Of the parents, 2 percent turned to prayer or divine help.

Another opinion on initial parental reaction is proffered by Zuk (1962), who pointed out that the three main emotional states or feelings experienced by a family when it discovered that a child was physically or mentally handicapped were disappointment, anger, and guilt.

In some instances, it is hard to categorize the parents' first reaction to a handicapped child because of the vagueness they feel at that time. Bice (1955)), in counseling parents of cerebral-palsied children, states that parents, when informed that their child has cerebral palsy, often report their first emotional response to be disappointment, but consider the term inaccurate to describe how they really feel. This vagueness on the part of many parents makes it questionable whether or not most parents are really conscious or aware of their first reactions to the discovery that their child is handicapped.

It should be stated for the sake of clarity that physical handicaps are not always recognizable at birth. Thus, it is noteworthy that a sizable group of parents never suspect their child to be handicapped until he has been a member of the family for some time. Barsch (1969), in a study of child rearing practices and cerebral palsy, states:

> While the child with cerebral palsy may be obvious to all at the age of five years, he is not obvious when he is only five months old. It is apparent that most parents become aware of handicaps only as expected behaviors do not emerge. It seems fair to conclude that most parents of handicapped children do not know they are the parents of a handicapped child for at least a year or more.

Ego involvements on the part of both parents help to determine the initial reaction to a handicapped offspring. These involvements often cause strong guilt feelings by parents, because they have been unable to produce what society considers to be the ideal child. Baum (1962) quotes Kozier's ideas on this narcissistic involvement of parents:

> In many ways, a child represents to the parent an extension of his own self . . . When the baby is born the mother's wish to be loved is partially transferred from her own person to that of the baby. To the father, a normal child is often an affirmation, at least in part, of his own sense of success. The capacity to produce unimpaired offspring is psychologically and culturally important for the parents sense of personal adequacy.

Research concerning the patterns of parental reaction to the physically handicapped offspring reaches a point of becoming abstract with respect to all the variables involved in determining these reactions. Many variables lending to the total reaction of the parent cannot be measured with a great deal of accuracy. The investigator must keep in mind that the initial reaction on the part of the parent is strictly individualized and is the result of his social, intellectual, emotional, and physical makeup. Other varied conclusions can be drawn of initial parental attitudes and are discussed later in this chapter.

Prolonged and Developmental Attitudes

The impact of the physically handicapped child on the family unit educes many different attitudinal patterns. These attitudes may be newly formed or merely more intensified examples of those parental emotions classified as "first reactions." For the sake of clarification, these two categories of parental attitudes will be referred to as *prolonged* and *developmental attitudes.*

Two distinct behavior forms, negative and positive, are readily visible within the prolonged and developmental attitudes and must be studied very closely in order to interpret the psychodynamic dilemma caused by the birth of a physically handicapped child.

In dealing with parental attitudes of a handicapped child, there seems to be an overfocusing on the idea that most parents are maladapted in their attitudinal approach to the child. Telford and Sawrey (1967) reinforce this idea by saying, "Because of our concern with the problem parents as well as the problem child, we can easily overlook the fact that many parents are able to cope in a healthy and constructive way with the problem presented by the presence of a defective child."

Barsh (1968) makes an observational opinion on the idea of *overfocusing* by saying, "The general tendency to characterize parents of handicapped children as guilt-ridden, anxiety-laden, overprotective, and rejecting beings is unfortunate. While it is true that such cases exist, the majority of the parents are unduly stigmatized by this generalization."

Rejection of the handicapped child appears to be very common among parents. These parents cannot adapt in a positive manner toward their child and, thus, exhibit an attitude of indifference or uninterest. In contrast to an indifferent attitude, many parents demonstrate their rejection in forms of anger or guilt feelings. The actual validity of parental rejection is hard to determine because rejection is generally an observed diagnosis by others instead of a confessed one by the parents. Hutt and Gibby (1965) help to substantiate the deduction that parental rejection is generally an observed characteristic: "Because the parent's rejection of the child is frequently unconscious, the parent is not aware of the basis of his own feelings toward him, and consequently he experiences severe conflicts."

In trying to select an adequate definition of parental rejection, it was discovered that Gallagher's (1956) is probably most functional: "The persistent and unrelieved holding of unrealistic negative values of the child to the extent that the whole behavior of the parent towards that child is colored unrealistically by this negative tone." Gallagher (1956) also divides parental rejection into two levels, the primary and the secondary rejection levels. In primary rejection, the cause of the negative attitude on the part of the parents is due to the basic, unchangeable nature of the child himself. Also, the dynamics that go to make up the personality of the parent, rather than the behavior of the child, often determine the attitudes of the parent. Secondary rejection, according to Gallagher, is the expression of negative attitudes due to the unfortunate behavior manifestations of the child himself.

There appears to be one specific point on which clinicians and educators seem to agree concerning attitude interpretation, and this is that parents have feelings of ambivalence toward the child. This appears to be the one common characteristic of almost all parents of a handicapped child. Telford and Sawrey (1967), in discussing these ambivalent feelings state:

> Even the best parents are ambivalent in their feelings toward their normal children. Parental attitudes, while dominantly positive, always have overtones of resentment and rejection. The restrictions of activities, the additional responsibilities, the minor disappointments of parenthood, the anxieties and the irritations which are a normal part of the bearing and rearing of offspring inevitably produce ambivalent parental reactions. Parents accept and love, but they also reject and dislike their children.

In further elaboration, Telford and Sawrey (1967) say that it is evident that the negative part of this ambivalence is much more intensified when the child is handicapped. These negative reactions vary from wishing the child had never been born to hidden and symbolic hostility and rejection. Nevertheless, ambivalent feelings cause guilt reactions, frequently resulting in oversolicitation, overprotection, and a life of parental martyrdom that constitutes an attempt to compensate for hostile feelings for which the person is ashamed.

Wrightstone (1957) says that parental attitude toward the offspring and the orthopedic limitations is ambivalent in nature. Although many parents are accepting in attitude, the acceptance is somewhat limited by the elements that may be distinguished as negative in effect. On the other hand, examples of warmth are often seen in parents who tend to reject their children. The amount of marital harmony in a marriage exemplifies a pronounced relationship concerning the attitude manifested toward the child. Parents who have a good marital relationship tend to accept, while those parents who have a poor relationship tend to reject their children.

Another attitude often demonstrated by the parents of physically handicapped children is denial. Denial is a defense mechanism that allows the parent to disavow the real disability of the child by simply refusing to acknowledge its existence. In most instances, denial is a form of escape. Telford and Sawrey (1967) think that, except for the most obvious defects, most parents deny the evidence of their child's inadequacy. There are many strong social and personal forces causing the parent to deny the disability in his child. The stereotype of the ideal child, the parents' hopes and aspirational desires for their children, the child as an extension of the parents' ego—all contribute to the "it just can't be true" reaction at the birth of a defective child. Because of the need of the parents to identify with the child, they invariably experience a loss of self-esteem at the birth of the child.

Attitude Change Effected Through Parent Counseling

Parental counseling involves many therapeutic and diagnostic processes. In counseling parents of the physically handicapped child, these processes are directed toward a goal of acceptance, adapting present behavior, and understanding of parental reaction. The parent-group and individual methods are very effective ways of dealing with the problems of most parents who have a defective child.

Thurston (1963), through his study of parents with cerebral-palsied children, was able to compile significant data concerning the attributes of the parent-group method of counseling. In response to the question "Are talks with other parents considered of value?" Thurston found that 86 percent of the responding parents answered positively, while only 7 percent replied in the negative. This indicated a ratio of about twenty-to-one in favor of the parent-group therapy. Thurston (1963) asserts that the reason for these positive replies is that, through the use of parent groups, the parents can learn to handle problems concerning their handicapped child, obtain personal relief from tension and guilt feelings, and meet other parents who understand.

Of the parents in Thurston's study who disapproved of parent meetings, 3 percent objected because they felt that the meetings "never solved anything"; 2 percent of those who replied negatively felt the meeting would be emotionally disturbing and would provide no benefits.

Love (1967), while in favor of the parent-group method, also criticizes it; there is often a preoccupation that the pathological will distort the parent's view of life and increase anxiety. It is also possible that parent groups are dominated by emotionally maladjusted parents who tend to disturb other members of the group further.

Today, in any counseling situation, the trend seems to be oriented toward emphasizing the parent-child relationship. Bennett (1958) noted that professional people claimed that parent-education programs were more effective when approached on a parent-child relationship basis instead of a child– or handicap-centered basis. Also in 1958, Mosher and Stewart said, "One of the most important factors to keep in mind in parent counseling is the quality of parent-child relationships."

Bennett (1958) probably best described the importance of the parent-child relationship to the development of the handicapped child:

> The kind of people his parents are and the kind of relationship he has with them matter more for the development of the child's personality and his mental health than the knowledge they possess. Deep-seated emotional attitudes to a handicap can be a greater barrier to the realization of potential in the handicapped child than in the handicap itself. 'Being told' or 'knowing better' appears insufficient to change such adverse attitudes, whether they are expressed in rejections of the handicap and the child, in rigidities in training techniques, or in over-solicitousness.

The Ideal Child

Parents develop certain expectations about a child before he is born, and often the unborn child becomes, in their minds, the ideal child. When a physically handicapped child is born, the mother is the hardest hit of the two parents. She feels that she has produced a defective child, while the father can stand off at a distance and use the defense mechanism of "denial" and pretend that the defect is no fault of his. However, as time passes, it turns out that the mother develops an accepting attitude toward the child faster than the father. In fact, whether the mother's attitude becomes one of acceptance with realistic perceptions or one of rejection, employing defense mechanisms, such as repression, projection, displacement, denial, and withdrawal, it will be clearly defined faster than the father's attitude because she is in constant contact with the child until his school days. The father often stands at a distance during the child's earlier years, his task of planning and providing for the child's future does not require close personal contact. However, the nature of the physical handicap (it is readily observable) often causes awareness of the child's problem by the parent on sight. This striking reality can force either parent to respond to the child with feelings, attitudes, and behavior that are unconsciously determined. He is not the ideal child.

In the area of research related to the attitudes of parents of physically handicapped children, it must be noted that only a limited number of valid studies have been attempted. Because of the lack of important precedential material, an acute diagnosis of parental attitude is impossible within the score of this chapter. Yet, some general observations of the problem can be made.

In analyzing initial reaction to the birth of a handicapped child, it can be concluded that most parents who have handicapped children have exhibited some type of initial reaction to the birth of the child. These reactions, although variant in intensity from parent to parent, can usually be classed as "common" or "normal" for individuals faced with this situation.

The prolonged or developmental attitudes are both positive and negative in nature and are expressed by the parents in the form of rejection, denial, or acceptance. Most parents, however, seem to be accepting in attitude toward their physically handicapped child.

In regard to parent counseling, it may be stated that, in most cases, there is a need for some type of counseling service that is both educational and rewarding in nature.

PARENTAL ATTITUDES TOWARD CHILDREN WITH SPECIAL HEALTH PROBLEMS

Children with special health problems have a variety of chronic ailments that confine them to bed for relatively long periods of time or curtail their activity periodic- or chronically.

In the search for information pertaining to parental attitudes toward these children, five reactions of parents were more common than others: (1) anxiety, (2) disbelief, (3) hostility, (4) helplessness, and (5) resentment.

A serious threat occurs to the set of values an individual establishes as a parent when a child in the family is sick for a long period of time. The dismay, the fear of the unknown concerning the condition in the child's future, and the feeling of helplessness combine to make the burden great. Often, parents cannot bring themselves to face the reality of this handicap. They try to keep the neighbors from knowing; they may neglect to seek the help they need; or they may go from one doctor to another, refusing to believe the diagnosis. Many times, they are really trying to find someone who will tell them that it is not as bad as they fear.

The term *special health problems* encompasses a multiplicity of conditions. Cardiac conditions, polyiomyelitis, cerebral palsy, spina bifida, malnutrition, epilepsy, diabetes, allergic disorders, anemia, tuberculosis, various crippling conditions, and leukemia are some of them. The common elements in all of these conditions include chronic illness, the need for continuing medical attention, and certain restrictions of activity necessarily imposed on the individual.

Although research has been conducted on the specific special health problems, there is little in the literature concerning the health problems. The available material deals more with the general topic of parental attitudes toward children with special problems. Parental attitudes toward all types of handicaps do not seem to be influenced by the causative factors or the severity of the handicap, as much as by the general adjustment of the parents. The better the parent's adjustment the more able he is to cope with the child's handicap.

When considering parental reactions to a special health problem, it is important to remember that, in some instances, these health problems develop after the child has lived a normal life for some period of time. Many of these children are normal at birth and their problem develops later. In some cases, the condition is apparent or at least suspected during infancy.

The Importance of Parental Attitudes

The child's adjustment to any of the special health conditions depends on the effects of the disease, extent of the chronicity, results of hospitalization, and effects on the family group. But the single most important factor related to the child's adjustment seems to be parental attitude.

Cardiac Child

When the cardiac child returns home from the hospital after a long absence, he feels that the parents have rejected him, often developing hostility toward the parents. Many parents do not prepare or help the child to adjust to his return home. They overprotect and overcontrol the child and often keep him from establishing favorable peer relationships. This separation from peers can cause the child to develop a fear of competition and of losing. The parents, in some cases, also use the threat of the possibility of a recurrence of a cardiac condition as a method of controlling aggressive behavior in the child.

Diabetic Child

Weller (1966) writes about the parents of the diabetic child. He states that whether the child's first manifestation of his condition is a severe diabetic coma or mild symptoms, the parents' first reaction to the knowledge that their child is diabetic is a reaction of shock. The initial shock subsides, and the parents realize that this is a permanent condition, one that they and their child will have to contend with for life.

Research indicates that fathers of diabetics appear to take the news better than mothers, who may become very resentful and disturbed concerning the problem. Often parents blame themselves for causing the condition in the child. This is particularly true if the parents know that this is a recessively inherited condition.

Muscular Dystrophic Child

The psychological reactions of parents of children with muscular dystrophy were studied by Solow (1965). He found the following:

1. Those parents who did not have proper understanding or acceptance of their child's condition were not able to help the child realize his own limitations.
2. When the child became ill and before his condition was diagnosed, anxiety built up in the parents.
3. Parents of children with muscular dystrophy want their children to attend school, because this relieves them of the problem of having to care for the child all of the time and

this prevents the "vegetation and isolation" of a child who would have to stay at home all of the time.

Asthmatic Child

The journals report several studies on the allergic complex, the exzema, hay-fever asthma complex. Two studies indicate that the asthmatic child is rejected by his mother. The mother seems too concerned with her own problems to give the proper amount of love and attention to the child. However, she often compensates for this by being overprotective. Asthmatic children seem to be overdependent, emotionally immature, and to have little self-confidence.

The asthmatic attack has a psychological basis. Newman (1955) states, "French and Alexander formulated their hypothesis that the psychological conflict in asthma is a repressed longing, basically for the mother. When this desire is frustrated or threatened with frustration, an asthmatic attack is precipitated. The asthmatic attack becomes symbolically the protest of a crying spell."

Several other studies found that the number of asthmatic children who suffered from overprotection was much higher than in a control group of nonallergic children.

Many mothers of asthmatic children avoid frustrating the child for fear that the frustration will cause an asthmatic attack. Newman (1955) says, ". . . the child's attacks are increased under emotional strain. This situation, of course, has important consequences in the parent's attitudes toward the child. Parental over-anxiety appears to be the rule. Asthmatic attacks thus can be precipitated not only by external factors, such as dusts, food, but by friction at home."

COUNSELING OF PARENTS

Harry and Ruth Bakwin (1967) state that parents can best be helped by an explanation of the nature of the illness and its probable outcome. One method of informing the parents is through parent groups. A number of parent groups have been organized at local, state, and national levels, generally on the basis of problems and interests common to parents of children with a particular handicap. These groups vary in the number of members, scope, and program, but Carr (1959) feels there is value in all such organizations. For one thing, the members help one another in sharing concerns; they are able to obtain information they want and need from speakers and professional resource persons; they give leadership in making their communities aware of the particular needs of their children and in meeting those needs.

According to a study made by Levy (1952), the parent groups appear to offer great help to their members in overcoming the feeling of isolation and the sense of frustration. This is attributed both by the professional observers and by the parents themselves to the release of tension resulting from discussion and activity directed toward the solution of problems. Perhaps most important is the encouragement that comes from knowing that one's problem is not unique.

Levy (1952) is also critical of some of the parent groups. "Constant preoccupation with the pathological is considered to distort the parents' viewpoint towards life and to increase rather than reduce anxieties . . . Others have pointed out that the parent groups may be dominated by persons who are themselves disturbed, tending to disturb others further."

In counseling the parents of handicapped children, the trend today seems to be toward emphasizing the parent-child relationship rather than child- or handicapped-centered. Bennett (1957) noted that, recently, professional people have claimed that programs designed to help the child through parent education could do so more effectively by an approach which was parent-child-relationship centered and, therefore, deeply concerned with the parent as a person.

In discussing the counseling of parents of handicapped children, Carr (1959) states, "The problems faced by the parents of a handicapped child are great, but through demonstrated courage and imagination of a high degree, their efforts to broaden their knowledge and understanding will do much to create a good life for their children."

REFERENCES

Bakwin, H. and Bakwin, R.M.: *Clinical Management of Behavior Disorders in Children.* Philadelphia and London, Saunders, 1967.

Barsch, R.H.: *The Parents of the Handicapped Child: The Study of Child Rearing Practices.* Springfield, Thomas, 1968.

Baum, M.H.: Some dynamic factors affecting family adjustment to the handicapped child. *Except Child, 28:*387, 1962.

Bennett, D.N.: Therapy with parents of handicapped children. *Except Child, 23:*154-155, 1957.

Bice, H.V.: Parent counseling and parent education. In Cruickshank, W.M. and Raus, G.M. (Eds.): *Cerebral Palsy — Its Individual and Community Problems.* Syracuse, Syracuse U Pr, 1955.

Carr, L.B.: Problems confronting parents of children with handicaps. *Except Child, 25:*225, 1959.

Gallagher, J.J.: Rejecting parents? *Except Child, 22:*273-274, 1956.

Hutt, M.L. and Gibby, R.G.: *The Mentally Retarded Child Development, Education, and Treatment,* 2nd ed. Boston, Allyn, 1965.

Levy, J.H.: A study of parent groups. *Except Child, 19:*22, 1952.

Love, H.D.: *Exceptional Children in a Modern Society.* Dubuque, Brown Pub, 1967.

Mosher, F.S. and Stewart, M.: Parents' expectations in planning for their childs' rehabilitation. *Except Child, 25:*120, 1958.

Newman, J.: Psychological problems of children and youth with chronic medical disorders. In Cruickshank, W. (Ed.): *Psychology of Exceptional Children.* Englewood Cliffs, P-H, 1955.

Solow, R.A.: Psychological aspects of muscular dystrophy. *Except Child, 32:*99-103, 1965.

Telford, C.W. and Sawrey, J.M.: *The Exceptional Individual: Psychological and Educational Aspects.* Englewood Cliffs, P-H, 1967.

Thurston, J.R.: Counseling the parents of the severely handicapped. *Except Child, 26:*351, 1960.

Thurston, J.R.: Attitudes and emotional reactions of parents of institutionalized cerebral palsied, retarded patients. *Am J Ment Defic, 68:*231-232, 1963.

Weller, C. and Boylan, B.R.: *The New Way to Live With Diabetes.* Garden City, Doubleday, 1966.

Wrightstone, J.W.: Studies of orthopedically handicapped pupils. *Except Child, 23:*164, 1957.

Zuk, G.H.: The cultural dilemma and spiritual crisis of the family with a handicapped child. *Except Child, 28:*405, 1962.

INDEX